THE REFLECTIVE PRACTICE GUIDE

The Reflective Practice Guide supports all students for whom the process of reflecting on developing knowledge and skills is crucial to successful professional practice. It offers an accessible introduction to a wide range of theories and models that can help you engage more effectively in critical reflection. Illustrated throughout with examples and case studies drawn from a range of interdisciplinary professional contexts, *The Reflective Practice Guide* offers models of practice that can be applied in a variety of settings. Reflective questions in each chapter help you apply ideas to your own professional context.

   Drawing on literature from a range of disciplines, key aspects of reflection explored include:

- becoming more self-aware
- the role of writing in reflection
- learning from experience
- learning from positives and negatives
- emotions and processing feelings
- bringing assumptions to the surface
- learning from feedback
- reflecting in groups
- managing change.

The Reflective Practice Guide is an essential source of support, guidance and inspiration for all students on education, nursing, social work and counselling courses who want to think about practice at a deeper level, question approaches, challenge assumptions and gain greater self-awareness.

Barbara Bassot is Senior Lecturer at the Centre for Career and Personal Development, Canterbury Christ Church University, UK.

THE REFLECTIVE PRACTICE GUIDE

An interdisciplinary approach
to critical reflection

Barbara Bassot

Routledge
Taylor & Francis Group

LONDON AND NEW YORK

First published 2016
by Routledge
2 Park Square, Milton Park, Abingdon, Oxon OX14 4RN

and by Routledge
711 Third Avenue, New York, NY 10017

Routledge is an imprint of the Taylor & Francis Group, an informa business

British Library Cataloguing in Publication Data
A catalogue record for this book is available from the British Library

Library of Congress Cataloging in Publication Data
Bassot, Barbara.
The reflective practice guide : an interdisciplinary approach to critical reflection / Barbara Bassot.
pages cm
Includes bibliographical references and index.
1. Nursing. I. Title.
RT41.B293 2016
610.73−dc23
2015017531

ISBN: 978-1-138-78430-7 (hbk)
ISBN: 978-1-138-78431-4 (pbk)
ISBN: 978-1-315-76829-8 (ebk)

Typeset in Interstate
by Swales & Willis Ltd, Exeter, Devon, UK

CONTENTS

1   What is reflective practice?   1

Introduction • Definitions • Why professionals need to reflect critically
• Preventing stagnation • Developing professional knowledge, skills and attitudes
• From unconscious incompetence to unconscious competence • The four
theoretical foundations of critical reflection • Tacit knowledge • From technical
rationality to reflection-in-action (Schön) • Making time to reflect
• A reflective space • The benefits of investing time in reflection • Conclusion

2   Becoming more self-aware   15

Introduction • The metaphorical mirror • How do I learn best? • Honey and
Mumford's learning styles • Strengths and allowable weaknesses • Developing
the Reflector style • SWOT/B and SWAIN analysis • Motivation • Transactional
Analysis drivers • Conclusion

3   The role of writing in reflection   31

Introduction • Why writing? • What is reflective writing?
• How to start writing reflectively • A structure for reflective writing
• Using a reflective diary or journal to aid professional growth • Is it all
about writing? • Conclusion

4   Experiential learning   42

Introduction • What do we mean by learning from experience?
• The ERA cycle • Kolb's experiential learning cycle • Reflection-on-action
• Driscoll's 'What?' model • Learning as transformation • Do we always learn
from experience? • Conclusion

5   Learning from positives and negatives: critical incidents   57

Introduction • What is a critical incident? • The problematic experience
• Learning from positive experiences • Conclusion

FIGURES

TABLES

PREFACE

For a number of years I have been privileged to teach a large number of students on programmes designed to prepare people for a role in the helping professions. My own professional area of career development and guidance is relatively small compared to others, such as nursing, teaching and social work. As a result, literature on reflective practice specifically related to my field was fairly sparse. In my early days of teaching I found that I had to look to a number of other academic disciplines and draw on their literature in order to ensure that my students were not hindered in the development of their knowledge and skills in this vital area. It became very clear to me that there was a wealth of rich material that we could learn from.

The Reflective Practice Guide is the culmination of many years of teaching. I wrote it in order to bring together a body of literature from a range of professions and have also included some work of my own. While books written for specific professions will always be very valuable, our knowledge will be limited if we never look outside of our own particular academic boundaries. I trust that this book will enrich your practice as you draw on the knowledge and experience of professionals and academics from a variety of disciplines, and that ultimately it will enable you to give your clients the support they need and deserve.

ACKNOWLEDGEMENTS

I would like to thank my family, friends and colleagues for their invaluable support whilst writing this book. In particular, I would like to thank Marc Bassot for his careful proof reading and Martin Bassot for his excellent work on the diagrams. I would also like to thank Mary Andall-Stanbury, Dawn Tickner, Jane Westergaard and Karen Williams for their advice on the case studies. Finally, I would like to thank all my current and former students, as without them I would not have been inspired to write this book.

Figure 6.3 is reproduced with kind permission from the Oxford Centre for Staff and Learning Development, Oxford Brookes University.

INTRODUCTION

The important role of reflective practice is well recognised in a wide range of professional areas, including education, health, management and social care. If you are a student on a professional undergraduate or postgraduate programme, you will no doubt be asked to undertake a module (or more) on reflective practice, where you will be expected to engage in the process of reflecting on your developing knowledge and skills. As research has developed in this area, many people have come to realise that reflecting on experience alone is not enough. To take a genuinely reflective approach you need to be able to think about your emerging practice at a deeper level, questioning your approach, engaging with your feelings, questioning your assumptions and gaining greater self awareness. This is commonly referred to as critically reflective practice.

There are many books written on the subject of reflective practice. Typically, books are written within a particular academic discipline, e.g. education (in particular teaching), health (in particular nursing), and social work. Your tutors will undoubtedly recommend books written by those in their own discipline, and you should certainly follow their recommendations. However, there is much to be learned when the boundaries of academic disciplines are crossed. A recent ESRC project, 'Critical Reflection in the Professions' examined how research can enable reflective practice to be taken further forward. One of the main aims of the project was to bring together academics from a number of different disciplines to discuss how critical reflection can be researched and taught more effectively, in particular across disciplines.

The aims of this book are twofold. First, it is the first book of its kind to take a specifically interdisciplinary approach, drawing on literature from a wide range of academic areas, including those mentioned above. Throughout the book, you will be introduced to a wide range of theories and models that can help you to engage in critical reflection on your studies and professional development. This will enable you to read outside your own particular academic discipline. For example, student teachers will be able to read extremely helpful approaches from nursing and vice versa; this will be new material for many. In addition, many professional practitioners now work in multi-professional contexts and an understanding of reflective practice from fields outside your own will also be very helpful.

Second, this is a practical book that will help you to engage in critical reflection. In each chapter there are a number of examples and case studies drawn from a range of professional contexts to illustrate how the models can be applied in a variety of settings as well as your own. In addition, there are reflective activities in each chapter to help you to apply the theories and models to your own professional development.

Throughout the book the term 'client' is used to refer to the people who you engage within your role as a professional practitioner. If this is not an appropriate term for your particular context, please feel free to use an alternative, such as patient or student.

The book has twelve chapters and takes you on a journey from reflective practice to critically reflective practice. Reflective practice encourages us to review our learning experiences in order to seek improvement – to make our work even better. Critically reflective practice asks us to engage with our emotional responses and to be prepared to challenge some of the assumptions we might be making about people and situations. Here, it is important to recognise that issues of power in professional relationships and within organisations are often at work.

Chapter 1 begins with definitions of what reflective practice is and examines the reasons why professionals need to reflect critically on their work and practice. It considers the three key areas of professional knowledge, skills and attitudes, followed by a discussion of the learning journey from unconscious incompetence to unconscious competence. Brookfield's (1995) four theoretical foundations of reflective practice are examined, as are the importance and dangers of tacit knowledge and reflection-in-action (Schön, 1983). The chapter then explores critical reflection as a choice and the need for busy professionals to make time to reflect in order to reap the benefits of investing time in it.

The focus of Chapter 2 is on self-awareness: a key aspect of beginning to practice reflectively. Becoming more self aware is an ongoing process; and the helpful concept of the metaphorical mirror through which practice can be critically evaluated is introduced. The chapter then moves on to explore the vital question 'How do I learn best?' and draws on Honey and Mumford's (2000) work on learning styles. The strengths and allowable weaknesses of the styles are explored, in particular how to maximise strengths and minimise allowable weaknesses. The chapter concludes with an exploration of the use of SWOT/B (Strengths, Weaknesses, Opportunities and Threats/Barriers) and SWAIN (Strengths, Weaknesses, Aspirations, Interests and Needs) analyses as tools for personal and professional development. This is followed by a discussion of theories of motivation and Transactional Analysis drivers.

Chapter 3 focuses on the role of writing in reflection; this often enables us to reflecting at a deeper level. However, writing reflectively presents many challenges and we often need help to know how to start. Some tools for reflective writing are presented, in particular the benefits of using a reflective diary or journal are explored.

The focus of Chapter 4 is on learning from experience and considers some seminal work; Kolb's (1984) learning cycle and Schön's (1983) reflection-on-action. It poses the question 'Is this enough?' and whether or not we always learn from experience. Two models that are easy to apply (the ERA model - Experience, Review, Action and Driscoll) are also explored. The concept of transformative learning is introduced and the chapter concludes with why we do not always learn from experience.

Chapter 5 asks us to consider which kinds of experiences we learn the most from – positive ones or negative ones – and presents two contrasting models of reflection. Many people advocate that we learn from critical incidents, sometimes called problematic experiences (Osterman and Kottkamp, 2004), whilst others argue that we need to focus on positive experiences (Ghaye, 2011).

By Chapter 6 we are at the half way point on our journey and begin to explore critical reflection in more depth. Here, we explore the area of engaging with emotions and feelings in professional practice and question whether or not professionals can be truly objective. The chapter highlights why personal feelings need to be processed and the perils of failing to do so. 'The Almond Effect' is introduced and the work of Gibbs (1998) and Boud, Keogh and Walker (1995) are highlighted.

Chapter 7 is all about bringing our assumptions to the surface so we can understand them and the ways in which they influence our professional practice. It considers what assumptions are, how they come about and how they can be questioned. The work of Brookfield (1995), Argyris' Ladder of Inference (1992) and Argyris and Schön's (1974) concept of double loop learning are considered as tools to help us to challenge our assumptions.

Most of the book before this point is about reflection as an individual activity. In Chapter 8 the focus is broadened to discuss the vital role of feedback in the learning process and learning from others in the context of professional development. Characteristics of good and poor feedback are explained and the role of critical friendship is highlighted. A model for effective supervision and the Johari Window as a feedback tool are explored.

Chapter 9 continues this theme with its emphasis on reflecting in groups, and includes useful strategies and exercises for the group context. It also considers how groups can be facilitated effectively.

Chapter 10 deals with a broad range of issues related to the management of change and the challenge of constant and often rapid change in professional practice. It highlights strategies for coping with change, whilst exploring some theoretical approaches from business and management (in particular the work of Lewin) that can help us understand change better and analyse our responses to it.

The focus of Chapter 11 is on critically reflective practice as a way of being. This involves being open to change, dealing with issues of vulnerability and taking a questioning approach to practice. The work of Johns is central to this chapter and a consideration of professional practice as artistry. The chapter also considers the possible benefits of 'mindfulness' strategies in helping professional practitioners to manage stress.

The book concludes with Chapter 12, which seeks to bring together many of the aspects of the book in an integrated model for reflection. It also considers Senge's concept of personal mastery and the importance of having a clear vision for our practice in order to generate the creative tension we need to keep moving forward. This emphasises the need to continue to learn throughout our professional lives.

I hope that this book will enable you to develop your knowledge and understanding of critically reflective practice and that it will help you in your personal and professional development as you seek to support others in your practice.

Barbara Bassot

1   What is reflective practice?

'Without reflection, we go blindly on our own way, creating more unintended consequences, and failing to achieve anything useful.'

(Margaret J. Wheatley, 2002)

Introduction

In this first chapter we will begin by examining some definitions of the term reflective practice and consider some of the reasons why professionals need to think critically about their work. We will examine the four theoretical foundations of critical reflection and explore the concepts of reflection-in-action and tacit knowledge. We will discuss issues of time management and the importance of making time to reflect. The chapter concludes with a focus on the many benefits of reflection.

Definitions

If you were to look in a standard dictionary for a definition of the word 'reflection', you would find at least two groups of words. The first refers to mirror images and the second to the act of deep thinking. In many respects this gives us very helpful clues in relation to what reflective practice is and what it involves. It can be likened to looking into a mirror to see our practice and ourselves more clearly and so give some serious thought or consideration to what we see.

So what is reflective practice? Lucas (1991) offers a useful definition when he argues that it involves a systematic enquiry to improve and deepen our understanding of practice. The use of the word systematic here implies far more than thinking about things, for example, whilst you are driving home. It suggests that it needs to be done in an organised way and to be undertaken in depth, in order to gain the maximum benefit from it.

Many people have their own ideas of what reflective practice is and how they would define it. For example, I have heard people say things like 'I know what reflective practice is. I reflect every day as I am driving home from work'. Of course, it is not for me to comment on the quality of someone's driving, but suffice it to say that deep reflection is not likely to happen while you are behind the wheel of a car! It is helpful to think about what reflection is not as well as what it is, and Thompson and Thompson (2008) offer some useful pointers in relation to this. For example, it is not just pausing for thought from time to time, or something just for students who can then forget about it when they start work. It is not something that you only do alone, as reflecting with others can be very helpful too (see Chapter 9). It is not a replacement for theory, but involves drawing on theory to enhance your understanding of practice; reflection, then, is a key means of applying theory to professional practice. Thompson and Thompson are clear to point out that all practice involves the application of theory and that we all need to beware of 'the fallacy of theoryless practice' (Thompson, 2000: 32).

Why professionals need to reflect critically

The definitions above show that the reflective process is a complex one. When reading published literature, certain key terms are not always defined clearly; indeed, the terms reflection, reflexivity and reflectivity are sometimes used interchangeably, which can be confusing. The aim of this book is to take you on a journey from reflective practice (which focuses on learning from experience in order to improve practice), to critically reflective practice with its focus on paying attention to your emotional responses and being prepared to challenge your assumptions and the things you take for granted in everyday working life. This involves examining our personal values and issues of power in the context of working relationships, which leads to a careful consideration of reflexivity.

Critical reflection is vital in professional practice for the following reasons.

Providing a space for deep thinking

If you are an emerging professional you are entering a world where the pace of life is fast and you can feel significant pressure to make decisions quickly. At times you may feel that time spent thinking something through is a luxury that you cannot afford, as distinct from time invested. However, taking time to analyse situations (what happened and why) can prevent mistakes occurring in the future and can help to build your confidence as you feel more secure in your ideas about your practice.

Evaluating and developing practice

Being a professional involves the need for you to review your practice in an ongoing way in order to keep your knowledge up to date and to continue to develop your professional skills. Professional practice is constantly changing and never static. Thankfully this means it is never boring!

Preventing stagnation

As you gain experience it is important to ensure that your practice does not stagnate, but remains vibrant and focused on the needs of the client. In a relatively short space of time it is easy to 'get stuck in a rut', doing things in a particular way because you have always done them that way. Johns (2004: 5) sums this up very well when he states that reflective practice is 'the antidote to complacency, habit and blindness'.

Striving for excellence

It is essential that all practitioners are competent and can carry out their role in an effective way. However, the word competent could imply that the professional practitioner is only 'good enough'. Many in professional practice wish to strive for excellence and reflective practice offers one key way in which this can be achieved.

Making practice creative

Creativity is one important aspect of excellence, and practising reflectively means that new ideas can be generated. Reflection stimulates creative thought processes by taking a questioning approach. This encourages you to 'think outside the box' in order to be innovative.

Self-awareness

A vital part of the reflective process is that you gain a clear understanding of the attitudes and values you bring to your practice. As human beings, we are not 'blank sheets'; we all have experiences (positive and negative) of life that we take with us to work. Being aware of our attitudes and values means either that we are better able to stand back from our own views, in order to put the needs of clients first, or we are more aware of issues of personal involvement and the need to refer a client on to someone who is better placed to support them. This level of self-awareness means being prepared to engage with our feelings and emotions.

Being slow to make assumptions

Each day the human brain has to process millions of messages in order to function. To do this effectively, the brain learns to group similar things together. Thankfully this means we do not have to think through every minor detail of our lives every day. The effect of this is that we all make assumptions about things and people on a regular basis. In addition, irrespective of where we live, we are all part of societies and cultures where certain things and particular people are valued more than others. Reflective practice helps us to question our assumptions and prevents us from accepting things at face value. It encourages a deeper examination of issues, which is vital when seeking to promote equality and social justice for clients.

Providing an aid for supervision

During the reflective process it is inevitable that, at times, you will become aware of issues that need to be discussed in the confidential and supportive environment of supervision. This could include things that surprise and challenge you ('I didn't realise I thought like that') and things that remind you of previous negative experiences in your own life ('that reminds me of . . .'). This can be uncomfortable, but time and space for such discussions can help to prevent 'burn out'. If you do not have access to supervision, a discussion with a trusted, experienced colleague can also be extremely helpful.

Providing a means for constructing professional knowledge

Students often marvel at the knowledge of experienced practitioners when they observe them whilst on work placements. These practitioners often cannot explain how they know things, and demonstrate Schön's (1983: 49) 'tacit knowing-in-action'. This professional knowledge includes a high level of self-knowledge and can be constructed through the process of reflective practice.

Case study 1.1

Sally has just started a course in physiotherapy and her tutors have encouraged her to reflect on her learning. She feels that everything is very new and, although she has always wanted to be a physiotherapist, she now feels that she has so much to learn that it is all a bit overwhelming. Speaking to some second year students, she can see that they felt the same way as her when they first started, but rather than just letting things build up she decides she wants to try and identify some time and space for reflection as she believes this will help her in her studies. Initially, Sally decides to set aside 20 minutes per week (two slots of 10 minutes) for reflection. Each week she carries out a different task that she sets for herself; sometimes she reads through her notes in the coffee shop and on other occasions she visits the library to browse through the books on the shelves. She finds that she enjoys the calming atmosphere of the library and starts to spend more time there. In the basement there are some rooms that no one seems to know about and she decides to go there regularly.

Developing professional knowledge, skills and attitudes

All professionals show aspects of their professional knowledge, skills and attitudes in their daily practice. When seeking to develop as a professional practitioner, it is important to understand the differences between these three areas in order to become fully rounded.

Knowledge

This comes in many shapes and sizes and is usually specific to a particular profession. It will be important for you to build your professional knowledge continuously in order to keep pace with the changes happening around you. Often professional knowledge can be categorised as follows.

- Theoretical – explanations of practice usually published by academics and practitioners. A theory is simply one person's (or a group's) explanation of what they see in practice, or, as Brookfield (2006: 3) states, 'A theory is nothing more (or less) than a set of explanatory understandings that help us make sense of some aspect of the world'. However, such theory should be tested or explored in some way through research, otherwise it simply remains someone's idea or assertion.

- Procedural – knowledge of processes, procedures and systems that structure and guide professional practice.
- Evidence based – using evidence from previous research to find out 'what works'.
- Tacit – things we know but cannot always explain in words.

Knowledge can be seen as the building blocks of professional practice. As professionals, people come to us for particular things because we have specific knowledge. For example, if I have a bad back, I would go and see my doctor. If I have a bad back because I have had an injury at work, I might also go and see a solicitor to make a claim for compensation. If you imagine your particular professional knowledge as the kind of solid wooden building blocks that very young children play with, it is easy to see that a beautifully constructed tower can easily fall apart by a careless younger brother or sister knocking it over. In the same way, our professional knowledge can easily crumple without reflection; indeed, reflection is the glue that holds the building blocks of our professional knowledge together.

Skills

Professionals use a broad range of skills in their practice; some are specific to their profession and some are more general. Here are some of the more general ones that all professionals need to develop.

- Communication – these include interpersonal skills (e.g. listening, asking open questions, rapport building) and written skills often carried out using ICT (e.g. writing case notes, reports).
- ICT (information communication technology) skills – these include updating databases, communicating by email, sending text messages and using the internet for research.
- Self-management and time management – many professionals work with a certain level of autonomy and need to be able to manage their own work by prioritising tasks and managing their time effectively.

In addition, there will be specific skills that you will need to develop that are vital for your own particular profession.

Attitudes

The word attitude is used to describe our ways of thinking about things, which in turn influences the way we do things. It goes without saying that professional practitioners need to foster positive attitudes, but what does this mean? Here are some words that describe a practitioner with positive attitudes towards their professional practice.

- Approachable.
- Patient.
- Calm.
- Supportive towards colleagues and clients.

- A good communicator.
- Well organised.
- On time.
- Hard working.
- Follows things through and does what they say they are going to do.
- Slow to make assumptions.
- Non judgemental.
- Committed to anti-discriminatory practice.
- Quick to respond and act.
- Reflective.

Your ongoing development in the areas above will demand a high level of self awareness and openness to feedback from others in order to ensure that you can identify your strengths and those areas that you need to continue to work on.

Reflective activity 1.1

Imagine you overhear some of your colleagues having a conversation about you. What would you hope they would be saying in relation to your knowledge, skills and attitudes?

From unconscious incompetence to unconscious competence

A competent professional has well developed knowledge, skills and attitudes. One well known and useful model (sometimes referred to as the conscious competence learning model, the conscious competence matrix or the conscious competence ladder) describes the journey that people make when learning something new from 'Unconscious Incompetence to Unconscious Competence'. The origins of the model are unknown and it has the following four steps.

1   Unconscious incompetence – this is where most learners start. They are unaware of their lack of knowledge and skill and, put simply, they do not know what they do not know.
2   Conscious incompetence – as the learner progresses they become much more aware of their limitations and start to recognise what they do not know and cannot do.
3   Conscious competence – as the learner continues to move forward, they become more knowledgeable and skilled and begin to apply their learning. Typically, the learner does this in a deliberate step by step way.
4   Unconscious competence – by this point the learner can perform well in their work without much conscious thought, as their knowledge, skills and attitudes become embedded in their practice.

The model is depicted in Figure 1.1.

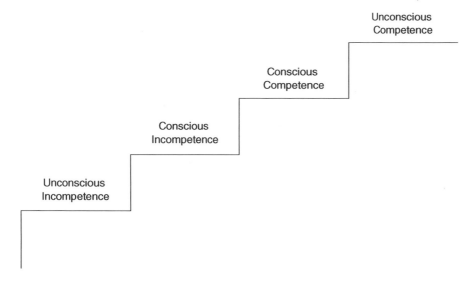

Figure 1.1 The conscious competence learning model

Whilst the model is very helpful and resonates with many people's learning experiences, the idea of professional practice at the fourth level without much conscious thought requires a note of caution. Such practice could easily run the risk of drifting back to the base of the model as we 'rest on our laurels' and bad habits set in. There can be a fine line between unconscious competence and unconscious incompetence and we need to be careful not to slip to the base of the model unconsciously, as shown in Figure 1.2 below.

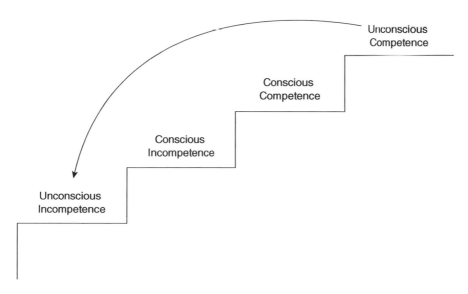

Figure 1.2 Slipping back to unconscious incompetence

Case study 1.2

Ben is training to be a primary school teacher and has just started his first placement. He respects and admires his mentor in school, and he feels lucky to have such good support, but finds it difficult to understand how and why she does certain things in her practice. He can see that she is a very skilful teacher, but often she cannot explain why she is doing what she is doing. She seems to put this down to intuition and sometimes even luck and often says to Ben things like 'I don't know why I did that' and 'I know, that was lucky, wasn't it?' Ben finds this frustrating, as he wants to learn how to become as good a teacher as he can. Instead of asking her how she knew which approach to take, he decides to ask her how she learned to approach a situation in a particular way. This helps Ben's mentor to realise how she has built her knowledge and skills over a period of time, which she is then happy to share with him.

The four theoretical foundations of critical reflection

When evaluating the relevance of critical reflection, it is important to understand its theoretical origins. Brookfield (2011) argues that there are four theoretical foundations that have informed critical reflection, which are as follows.

> **Analytic Philosophy** – as human beings we have the capacity to be logical, to distance ourselves from the way things are usually done and to exert some conscious control over our thoughts and actions. This is often described as reasoning – seeing the different sides of an argument and reaching sound conclusions.
> **Natural Sciences** – this is our capacity to look at a phenomenon and to try to explain it. For example, we have a hypothesis that we test by experiment, and through this process our hypothesis is either confirmed or refuted.
> **Critical Theory** – power dynamics are present in all situations and critical theory helps us to understand how these manifest themselves. It helps us to recognise hegemony – this is when we are deceived, even manipulated, into accepting the dominant ideology as being in everyone's best interest, even when this serves to work against certain groups of people, usually those without power and therefore on the margins of society.
> **Pragmatism** – this involves having a strong need to be open to constant experimentation, to explore new and better ways of doing things. This results in discovery and change.

Reflective activity 1.2

Think about the four theoretical foundations and write some notes on the evidence you can see in your own profession for each of these. Are some more dominant than others?

Tacit knowledge

As mentioned on page 4, students often marvel at the knowledge of experienced practition-ers when they observe them whilst on work placements. Very experienced practitioners often cannot explain how they know things and demonstrate Schön's (1983: 49) 'tacit knowing-in-action', sometimes referred to as tacit knowledge. When asking such profes-sionals why they did certain things in certain ways, many will reply 'I don't know – I just did it that way' or 'It just seemed right at the time'. This can lead to common misunderstand-ings about tacit knowledge. It would be easy to assume that the practitioner's response is based on intuition. However, being able to reach such conclusions quickly, almost on the spur of the moment, will undoubtedly have been learned through many past experiences. For example, none of us can say that we have always known how to be a good nurse, teacher or social worker. We have learned it. This is an important point because if this is not the case, then anyone could do what we do without any training, which undermines our knowledge and skills as professional practitioners. Just because we cannot always explain why we do things in words does not mean they are intuitive or simple. Some pro-fessions (for example career guidance and teaching) have suffered as a result of those with power thinking that given a simple set of instructions, anyone can do the work. This is simply not the case and, as professionals, we all need to beware of the danger of minimis-ing the nature of our tacit knowledge.

From technical rationality to reflection-in-action (Schön)

In his seminal publication *The Reflective Practitioner*, Schön (1983) discusses the concept of reflection-in-action in some depth. All of us spend time thinking – it is so much part of our everyday lives that sometimes we do not even realise we are doing it. Reflection-in-action is the kind of thinking we all do as we are working, studying and living generally, and as human beings we all have a capacity to think as we are doing other things. When writing about reflection-in-action, Schön (1983: 54) describes it as 'thinking on your feet'.

This type of reflection is very important for people who work with people, or as Schön would say, people in the minor professions. Such people cannot rely on the laws of science (what he calls technical rationality) to give them logical solutions to everyday problems. Because people are unique, there is no single response or action that will suit every situation. When working with clients it will often be necessary to try a number of different strategies to enable them to engage with the process. By reflecting-in-action, you will be able to assess the strategies you are using as you go along, deciding whether or not your approach is working with that particular individual or group. If not, you can change your approach and in many (but not all) cases find something that will work, or will at least work more effectively.

Reflection-in-action, like all reflection, is a skill that develops with practice. At first it is very difficult to concentrate on listening to the client, applying a theoretical model or approach, being sure to follow important procedures and thinking about what you are doing at the same time. Thankfully, practice makes perfect (well, better anyway!)

There are clear parallels here with learning to drive. At first it seems impossible to remember everything (mirror, signal, manoeuvre, etc.) But in time, and with good constructive feedback, things begin to fall into place. The day of the test arrives, and things go well. Congratulations! Of course, we know that now bad habits can set in, and this points to the dangers of relying on reflection-in-action only. This also serves as a reminder of 'the fallacy of theoryless practice' (Thompson, 2000: 32) when we might be fooled into thinking that we could do this all along.

Making time to reflect

As mentioned in the list of attitudes, being organised is vital for professional practice, and effective time management is an important skill that all professionals need to continue to work on. In my experience, time management is rather like fishing by hand – one day I think I've got it and the next it slips away from me! If there were one simple model that would guarantee that I could always manage my time well, then someone would have thought of it, published it and made millions, and hopefully that person would have been me! Meanwhile, visit any bookshop or browse on the internet and you will find lots of different books on time management. If you find one that helps you, use it, but don't become a slave to it, as it may not work for you forever.

One important theme in time management literature is recognising the difference between the important and the urgent. Being able to differentiate between these two concepts will undoubtedly be a key factor in achieving success in your professional life. Here are definitions of the two terms.

> *Urgent* – things that demand our immediate attention and at least give us the impression that they need to be done now.
> *Important* – things that help us to achieve our long-term goals.

Covey (2004) presents a useful model to help us to make this important distinction. This is represented by a square with four quadrants, which can be described as follows.

> *Quadrant 1 (top left)* – things that are both important and urgent. These are things that demand our immediate attention. They need to be done now and are often key elements of our job.
> *Quadrant 2 (top right)* – things that are important, but not urgent. Things in this quadrant tend to be more long term and do not need to be done now. However, they are very important to us and are often linked to things that we want to achieve as professionals.
> *Quadrant 3 (bottom left)* – things that are urgent but not important. It is easy to be deceived into thinking that everything that appears urgent is urgent, but this is often not the case. Sometimes things appear urgent because they are important to other people, particularly managers.

Quadrant 4 (bottom right) – things that are neither important nor urgent. We could say that such things should not be part of professional life, but we can easily slip into them when we feel 'swamped', tired and overloaded.

Many professionals spend a lot of time (if not too much time) in Quadrant 1. Covey is clear about the consequences of this, which include a range of symptoms caused by high levels of stress, feeling that you are constantly 'fire fighting' and managing crises; here the risk of 'burn out' is high.

Spending lots of time in Quadrant 3 is also something to beware of, as here you run the risk of being a 'slave' to the priority of others – in other words, focusing on things that are important for others but not for you. Your manager or those who are making demands on your time say 'jump' and you respond with 'How high?' Again, the risks here are high as you begin to see your own goals and plans disappear and become pointless, as you rarely achieve them. Your focus is on the short term and you begin to feel worthless and even victimised as your work spirals out of control.

Quadrant 4 is full of procrastination, often called 'the thief of time'. Here, time is stolen from us because we drift and put things off that we know we should be doing, and sometimes even things that we want to do. We do this for a range of reasons that are often personal to us and these can include:

- Fear of failure, or even fear of success.
- Not knowing where to start.
- Being so overwhelmed by the volume of work that we are experiencing that we cannot see a way forward.
- Boredom and lethargy.

Perhaps it is difficult to imagine professionals in Quadrant 4 as it is contrary to many of the professional attitudes we looked at earlier in this chapter. However, it is important not to be deceived by things that appear as legitimate work tasks, which can conspire against us if we are not careful. For example, the feeling that we need constantly to check emails to be sure we are up to date and not letting others down. Checking messages that do not apply directly to our work can waste many hours, for example when colleagues have clicked the 'reply all' button – something that we ourselves can avoid and only use when absolutely necessary to protect our colleagues.

Covey advocates spending a significant amount of time in Quadrant 2 where our own goals and priorities are in focus. Here, we are clear about what we hope to achieve in the longer term: such tasks and projects do not need to be done now, but they will help us to achieve our long-term goals. Much of this clarity comes from reflection and spending time thinking through what you hope to achieve will be important, particularly when it comes to managing large pieces of work. Remember too that taking time to reflect is a choice. However, if we spend too much time thinking about our long term goals, over time these will shift into Quadrant 1 as time runs out on us. What was previously 'not urgent' then becomes so as deadlines loom. Or worse, we fail to achieve them as we minimise their worth and they 'fall off the end'.

Case study 1.3

Rajesh is a student social worker who is beginning to feel that he needs to be more organised in his approach to his studies. On his Access course at college, most things were organised for him by his tutors and he could always go to them for support whenever things became difficult. He has moved away from home and knows that he needs to be an independent learner if he is going to succeed on his course. He decides to attend a time management course offered by the university's study support centre and can see that there are a lot of people like him, which is comforting. In addition he devises some strategies that he feels will help him; in particular, making sure that all his regular commitments (lectures, seminars and tutorials) are prioritised and itemised in his diary. This helps him to look at the rest of the time he has for reading and volunteering. In addition, Rajesh decides to ask for a peer mentor – a student in the year above him who can give him some support when he feels he needs it.

Avoiding distractions

When life is very busy it is all too easy to be distracted, and, before we even realise, we have wasted precious time on activities that might appear urgent, or that we have deceived ourselves into thinking could be important. If we are not careful, we have then lost our time for reflection. Here are some ideas for protecting our time.

- Get into the habit of blocking out a short amount of time in your diary – this need not be a big amount. You will be surprised how much you can achieve in 15 minutes per week.
- Do not let things interfere with your plans and see the time you have blocked out as time for your personal and professional development.
- Turn your phone off or turn it to silent if you do not feel you can turn it off. Only answer it if you know the call is genuinely urgent.
- Turn off your email. Most people can wait 15 minutes for a reply, and if not they will call you.
- Do not be afraid to ask people for a few minutes. Most people will understand if you are busy doing something important.

A reflective space

As well as making time to reflect, many people find having a reflective space is also important. This can help if, like many practitioners, you find it difficult to 'switch off' from work and activity. A space that you have identified as somewhere offering you the opportunity to focus on your development can be extremely helpful. Here are some examples of reflective spaces.

- A room at home where you can relax and not be distracted.
- A quiet spot in the library.
- A corner in your local coffee shop.
- A bench in your local park.
- A walk through the town or countryside.
- The quiet coach on a train.

It is important to understand that this space will be different for different people and the key is finding what suits you best; this is a key theme that will occur many times in this book. Of course, not everyone needs or indeed wants quiet in order to reflect; some of us do our best thinking with life's regular hustle and bustle around us. If that is you, do not be tempted to conform, but do what suits you best.

Case study 1.4

Emma, who has just started a degree in counselling coaching and mentoring, understands that she needs to take a reflective approach to her studies and her future work with clients. Emma decided to do the course because she gets on so well with people. At school, many people loved to talk to her because she is such a good listener and Emma liked the fact that people used to single her out as a good person to share their troubles with. Emma is living in a busy hall of residence and is already finding that people knock on her door when they need someone to talk to. This is fine, but it often means that Emma's room is a place for sharing, not somewhere where she can have any time to herself. She knows that she needs to find some space away from her room where she will be able to reflect on her development. After trying several different places, she finds a space in the corner of one of the busy coffee shops where she can blend in with the people around her. She also knows that the time will come where she will need to be kind but assertive in order to protect her time for reflection.

The benefits of investing time in reflection

There are many benefits from investing time in reflection and the case study below illustrates some of these.

Case study 1.5

Jackie is a second year nursing student and is in the early part of a placement on an adult general surgery ward. She is finding the workload very demanding as the ward is very busy and she is still often unsure about procedures. She is also aware that often things have to be dealt with quickly and efficiently in order to ensure that theatre time-tables are adhered to and surgeons are not kept waiting. Jackie often feels nervous about the possibility of making mistakes and knows that when she feels anxious she is more likely to make errors. Jackie decides to set aside 15 minutes after each shift to reflect on what she has learned and to discuss this with her mentor.

It is very easy in professional practice to become overwhelmed by the amount of things to learn and by a fear of making mistakes. Regular times for reflection helped Jackie in both of these areas of difficulty. She found being a student nurse and fitting into a busy ward to be a demanding and intense experience. Spending time reflecting meant that she could go over some of the procedures in her head and on paper; this helped her to build her confidence and, as a result, she was less likely to panic.

There are many more benefits of investing time in reflection, which will become evident as this book progresses. It is always worth noting that any time spent in reflection is time invested not wasted.

Conclusion

In this chapter we have examined some definitions of reflective practice and the reasons why professionals need to think critically about their work. We have looked at the four theoretical foundations of critical reflection and have explored the concepts of reflection-in-action and tacit knowledge. Throughout, the emphasis has been that critical reflection is a choice and that professionals need to make time to reflect in order to reap the many benefits from it. In the next chapter we move on to look at the whole area of self-awareness in relation to professional practice.

References

Brookfield, S.D. (2006) *The Power of Critical Theory for Adult Learning and Teaching*, Maidenhead: Open University Press, McGraw-Hill Education.

Brookfield, S.D. (2011) 'Critical Reflection' paper presented at ESRC Critical Reflection in the Professions: the Research Way Forward seminar, Birmingham, June 2011.

Covey, S. (2004) *The 7 Habits of Highly Effective People*, London: Pocket Books.

Johns, C. (2004) *Becoming a Reflective Practitioner*, 2nd edn, Oxford: Blackwell Publishing.

Lucas, P. (1991) 'Reflection, new practices and the need for flexibility in supervising student teachers'. *Journal of Further and Higher Education*, 15 (2), 84–93.

Schön, D.A. (1983) *The Reflective Practitioner*, Aldershot: Ashgate.

Thompson, N. (2000) *Theory and Practice in Human Services*, Maidenhead: Open University Press, McGraw-Hill Education.

Thompson, S. and Thompson, N. (2008) *The Critically Reflective Practitioner*, Basingstoke: Palgrave Macmillan.

Wheatley, M.J. (2002) It's an interconnected world. Available from www.margaretwheatley.com/articles/interconnected.html. Accessed 7 May 2015.

2 Becoming more self-aware

'Those of us who attempt to act and do things for others or for the world without deepening our own self-understanding . . . will have nothing to give others.'

(Thomas Merton, 1971)

Introduction

In the previous chapter we established that reflective practice involves examining ourselves to see our practice more clearly and giving some serious consideration to what we see. This will ensure that our practice grows and develops and that we do not stagnate. Becoming more self-aware is a crucial part of practising reflectively and this chapter introduces you to the concept of the metaphorical mirror: a vital tool for reflection in both senses of the word. We will explore the different kinds of mirrors that we use in our everyday lives to see what these can teach us about different aspects of reflective practice. We will then move on to consider how we learn best; learning and reflection go 'hand in hand' and it is difficult to imagine one without the other. It is important to remember that reflection is a skill, so it is something we can develop and improve upon. We will examine Honey and Mumford's (2000) learning styles and consider the strengths and weaknesses in the four styles and apply this to our own learning. The chapter continues with SWOT/B (Strengths, Weaknesses, Opportunities and Threats/Barriers) and SWAIN (Strengths, Weaknesses, Aspirations, Interests and Needs) exercises to help you to analyse your current position. The final sections examine issues of motivation and the role of drivers in helping us to understand more about what we do and why.

The metaphorical mirror

In my own professional practice with students I have often likened reflective practice to looking in a metaphorical mirror. Over time your practice will develop through a process of thinking and examining yourself and your actions. This will increase and deepen your levels of critical evaluation, helping you to gain greater self-awareness.

Looking in a variety of mirrors is an everyday occurrence for most people; we look in a mirror and then decide whether or not to take action on what we see. In this section we consider a range of different types of mirrors and the insights these can give us in relation to developing professional practice. Here are some examples of the kinds of mirrors we use regularly and the particular insights they give us into reflective practice.

- *The bathroom mirror* – most of us get up in the morning and, before long, look in some kind of mirror, often the bathroom mirror. Of course, we do not always like what we see! We then make a choice – we can decide to do nothing, or to take some action to make ourselves more presentable to the outside world! This simple example teaches us two important lessons in relation to reflective practice. First, when we start to reflect we may not always like what we see about ourselves and our practice. Taking action following reflection always involves choice; we can accept what we see as 'good enough', take no action and continue as we were. Or we can take action in order to improve and develop ourselves.
- *The full length mirror* – we use this kind of mirror when we want to see a full picture of ourselves, for example when trying on an outfit for a special occasion. Here we look at ourselves as a whole to see how the component parts of our outfit go together, for example whether our shoes match the rest. At times we need to examine our practice in this way, taking a holistic approach to situations, looking at the whole as well as the parts within it.
- *The 360° mirror* – these mirrors enable us to see from all angles, thereby giving us views of ourselves that we do not usually see. This reminds us that reflective practice is not merely a solitary activity and that the views of others are important when seeking to gain a full picture of ourselves.
- *The driver's mirror* – this is a vital tool that people use every time they get into the driving seat of a car. Using this mirror means we can see what is behind us and assess whether or not it is safe to move ahead; we learn to use it frequently when driving. Moving forward (for example to overtake) is dangerous without looking back first. This mirror reminds us that reflective practice involves looking back on experiences we have had, so that we know how to move forward.
- *Wing mirrors* – these also enable us to see what is behind us when driving. Some wing mirrors are convex in shape to give a wider view, others have a small magnifying mirror in one corner: both help us to see what is out of view just over our shoulder. This is a reminder that feedback from others plays a vital part in helping us to identify what we cannot see ourselves.
- *The magnifying mirror* – this is indispensable in situations where we need to look at our faces closely, for example when shaving, applying make-up or learning to use contact lenses. It helps us when we need to see things in fine detail. At certain times we need to examine our practice in this way, particularly if we are learning something new or if our decisions are challenged. There is also much to be gained from a close examination of an incident (often referred to as a critical incident), so that mistakes and pitfalls can be avoided in the future.
- *Funfair mirrors* – these mirrors distort what we see; obviously we do not look in these regularly. However, like the fun fair mirror, some practitioners and students can have

a distorted view of their practice. Some may always feel that what they did was fine because they did their best in the circumstances within the resources available to them; others can be very hard on themselves, always thinking that they could have done much better; this is sometimes referred to as the 'inner critic' (Williams and Penman, 2011). In both cases it is likely that there is some kind of distortion at work in the process. This again points to the vital role of feedback from others and discussion in order to get a more accurate picture of the situation.

- *Shop windows* – clearly these are not mirrors per se, but are places where we can see our reflection. Usually we look in these as we are walking along, and they remind us of Schön's (1983) concept of reflection-in-action and our ability to think while doing other things.

It is important to remember that all types of mirrors can quickly become 'steamed up' or dirty and need to be wiped down so they continue to fulfil their purpose. In the same way, we need to polish our metaphorical mirror regularly by checking what we see through our own individual thoughts and by being open to receiving feedback from others whom we trust. Otherwise we can easily be deceived into thinking that 'we look all right really' when our view of ourselves might be cloudy or even distorted.

How do I learn best?

Learning is a vital part of professional practice; this is not restricted to students in training and, as a result, many professional bodies have Continuing Professional Development (CPD) requirements to ensure that practitioners are keeping up to date and are continuing to develop their skills. Osterman and Kottkamp (2004: 24) make the important link between learning and reflection when they state that 'While experience is the basis for learning, learning cannot take place without reflection'. It is important to understand how we learn best as individuals so that we can maximise our learning. In this regard, recognising your learning styles can offer important insights into your ongoing development.

Honey and Mumford's learning styles

Several writers have focused on the concept of learning styles and the approach selected here is that of Honey and Mumford (2000) because of their interest in how people learn in organisational settings: in other words, how people learn at work. It is important to understand that Honey and Mumford see these styles as learning habits, so these are not things we are born with, but approaches that as individuals we have found to be effective through our experiences of learning over the years. Based on the work of Kolb (1984), they identified the following four different styles.

- **Activist**
  Activists are doers and like to be involved in new experiences. They tend to take an unbiased approach and are focused on the present. They are open-minded, tend not to be sceptical, and have lots of enthusiasm. They enjoy getting on with the task in hand and

can achieve a lot in a relatively short space of time. They often act first and think things through later and can become bored quickly, particularly in relation to the implementation of longer-term projects.

- **Reflector**

  Reflectors are thoughtful people who like to stand back and observe people and situations from a variety of angles. They enjoy collecting data before reaching any conclusions. This means they tend to be cautious and can be slow to make decisions. They can often suffer from procrastination. In meetings they will often be quiet, but when they do speak their arguments will usually be well thought through. They take into account 'the bigger picture', including past experiences as well as the views of others.

- **Theorist**

  Theorists are analytical people who enjoy integrating their observations into complex and logically sound theories. They think problems through in step-by-step ways and are interested in systems and processes. They tend to be perfectionists who like order and prefer schemes that are rational. They are objective and can be detached, rejecting ideas that do not fit with their tried and tested approaches. They can get 'bogged down' in detail and can feel uncomfortable with taking a more subjective approach if it is needed.

- **Pragmatist**

  Pragmatists like to try out ideas to see if they work in practice. They like to experiment and find new ways of doing things to see if they will be more effective. They are practical, 'down to earth' people who see a problem as a challenge they would like to solve. They enjoy planning but can become cynical and reject ideas that have been tried in the past and been seen to fail. They can be impatient with long discussions and want to act quickly and confidently to move things forward.

Most people have a tendency to have a preference for more than one style. In my experience of using the Learning Styles Questionnaire with students, many of those who have strengths in the Activist style also score highly on the Pragmatist style. The same tends to apply to those with strong Reflector and Theorist styles. However, this is not always the case.

Reflective activity 2.1

Having read the descriptions above, which style or styles do you feel describes you best and why? Now think about which are least like you and why.

Strengths and allowable weaknesses

It is clear from the descriptions above that there are many strengths associated with each of the four learning styles. However, when any of the styles are 'overdone' they can easily become a weakness, often termed an allowable weakness. Table 2.1 illustrates this.

Table 2.1 Strengths and allowable weaknesses

Learning style	Strength	Allowable weakness
Activist	• Quick to respond • Enthusiastic to start • Focused on action • Achiever • Open minded • Good leaders • Keen to volunteer	• Too quick to respond • Loses enthusiasm quickly • Doesn't take time to think things through • Prone to making mistakes • Often has to re-do things slightly differently because of lack of forethought • Impatient with others • Can get in 'over their head'
Reflector	• Thoughtful • Good listener • Patient • Sees the viewpoints of others • Sees the 'big picture' • Creative • Makes few mistakes	• Over-thinks • Slow • Procrastinates • Non committal • Can become 'paralysed' when there are lots of options • Prone to panic when a speedy response is needed • Indecisive
Theorist	• Analytical • Logical and objective • Eye for detail • Perfectionist • Organised • Good manager	• Over analytical • Rejects things that do not appear to 'fit' • Lacks spontaneity • Denies value of subjectivity • 'Nit-picky' • Over-organises • Finds it hard to know when things are good enough
Pragmatist	• Practical • 'Down to earth' • Good at planning • Forward looking • Keen to experiment and try out new ideas • Confident • Problem solvers	• Not as interested if cannot see how something will work in practice • Can spend too much time planning • Not flexible when things don't go according to plan • Cynical if an idea has been tried before and not worked • Critical of theory • Impatient in long discussions • Too much focus on task rather than people

Reflective activity 2.2

Look back on what you wrote in the previous activity. Which strengths and allowable weaknesses do you feel apply to you and which do not? Can you think of any others that have not been included?

> **Case study 2.1**
>
> Amit is training to be a secondary school teacher in science. When he examines his learning styles he recognises straight away that he has a strong Theorist style, shown by his love of solutions and models that give him a correct answer. However, learning to teach is a very different experience for Amit, and whilst on placement he soon realises that where the science he loves gives him a correct answer, the students he is working with seem to learn in different ways. He tries lots of different approaches when explaining key concepts but only some students seem to grasp what he is trying to put across. Amit begins to understand that he needs to spend time reflecting on how his students learn in order to select the most appropriate teaching methods, particularly for those students who are not responding well to his current approach. He also realises that his own students exhibit a range of different learning styles and, following a discussion with his mentor, he decides to discuss this with them in tutorial time.

It is important to emphasise that the notion of strengths and allowable weaknesses in relation to learning styles should not serve to categorise people. So, for example, because I am a Reflector, this does not mean that I am generally slow – rather that if I overdo it, I will have a tendency to be slow. If I am a Theorist, this does not mean that I will always overanalyse situations, but that I might have a tendency to do so. Knowing our learning styles means that we can focus on our strengths and avoid or minimise our allowable weaknesses.

Two particular viewpoints dominate when considering Honey and Mumford's learning styles.

First, if I know my styles, I can select experiences that best suit my style and deselect those that do not. The danger with this approach is that it could restrict my learning and, of course, I will not always be in a position to make this selection. At times I may have to step outside the 'comfort zone' of my preferred style or styles.

Second, if I want to maximise my learning, understanding my allowable weaknesses and my least preferred styles gives me clear pointers regarding things to work on in my professional development. If I have strengths in all the styles this means I am likely to be a strong, all round learner, open to developing in all areas of my professional practice.

Developing the reflector style

If you are a student on a programme of professional education or a professional practitioner, it will be important to develop your Reflector style. If you feel that you do not have strengths in this particular area, here are some examples of things you can do to help you become more reflective.

- If you tend to rush into situations, practice 'holding yourself back'. You can do this by making sure that you wait for others to respond first before giving your views. If you need to, you can 'buy yourself some more time' by saying something like 'I'm tempted to respond straight away, but know I should take a bit of time to think about this to stop me rushing into things'.

- Practice observing people in meetings. Notice how different people behave, how much they contribute to discussions and what they have to say. Review this and also think about your own contributions.
- Practice listening in meetings and in conversations – again, try not to be the first person to respond, particularly to requests.
- Practice looking at things from different perspectives. Write down how you see a situation and then how others involved might see it.
- Spend a regular short amount of time (e.g. 15 minutes) writing about your experiences (see Chapter 3). Read what you have written each week or month to see how you are making progress.
- Find a 'critical friend' (see Chapter 8) and share how you are getting on.

Case study 2.2

Gabrielle is a trainee paramedic who is progressing quite well on her course. During her time on placement she recognises that she has a tendency to want to act swiftly (an important quality for a paramedic), but has recently found on a couple of occasions that this has led to some tricky consequences, having rushed into saying things to a patient too quickly to try and put them at ease. Her mentor has pointed out the need for her to slow down and to be calm and thoughtful in her approach. Gabrielle has recognised that she has a strong Activist style and that she loves to take action quickly to help people. However, she realises that this is where mistakes can happen and is keen to slow herself down to ensure that her mistakes are kept to a minimum. Gabrielle decides to take some conscious steps to listen to the patient more carefully and to observe how her mentor approaches situations. She remembers that she still has a lot to learn and that a calm paramedic is likely to be a good paramedic.

SWOT/B and SWAIN analysis

Becoming more self-aware often means being prepared to engage in a level of self-analysis. Here are two tools that can help you to achieve this.

SWOT/B analysis

A SWOT analysis is a tool often used in business to critically evaluate a range of aspects related to a piece of work or project. It can also be used individually to help you to analyse yourself as you seek to understand your current position and how you could move forward in your professional development. In this context, strengths and weaknesses are internal and opportunities and threats are external. Some writers replace Threats with Barriers, hence SWOT becomes SWOB. Barriers to learning can be internal (for example, lack of confidence or self-belief) or external (for example, a noisy hall of residence or student flat). You can use the tool effectively by posing the following questions.

Strengths

What am I good at and where do my talents lie?
What do I find easy?
What do I enjoy?
Where do I have expertise?
How have I excelled in the past and which of my achievements am I most proud of?

Weaknesses

Where am I most likely to have difficulties and why?
What do I dislike?
What do I struggle with?
What would I like to do better?
What do I put off doing?

Opportunities

What opportunities are there for my development?
What could I do to gain more skills?
What could I do to become more confident in my weakest areas?
Who can I ask for support?
Who can I find to act as my mentor?

Threats/Barriers

What will hinder my development?
What obstacles do I face in my development?
What or who might discourage me?
How can I prevent this happening?
What strategies can I put in place to try to ensure my success?

Following the completion of a SWOT/B analysis, you can then continue to develop your strengths, work on your weaknesses, make the most of your opportunities and seek to minimise the threats and barriers.

SWAIN analysis

This is another tool for self analysis, where, as well as identifying your strengths and weak-nesses, you are also asked to think about your aspirations, interests and needs. Here are some further questions.

Aspirations

Where would I like to be in a year's time?
In three years?

In five years?

When I look back on my working life, what would I like to be able to say I have achieved? What might be my greatest achievement?

Interests

What do I love doing?

What do I have a real passion for?

What gives me energy?

If I could spend all my time at work doing one thing, what would that be?

What would I really struggle to give up?

Needs

What do I need to do to succeed?

What training do I need?

Do I need further qualifications and if so which?

What knowledge and skills do I need to develop?

Do my ways of thinking need to change and if so, how?

Case study 2.3

Paul is a newly qualified counsellor and his supervisor has encouraged him to undertake an analysis of his strengths and areas for development. Paul decides to use a SWOT/B analysis and also to consider his aspirations, interests and needs.

Strengths	*Weaknesses*
• Listening skills • Empathy • Dedication • Commitment	• Becoming too involved with clients • Wanting to protect clients rather than enable them • Showing sympathy • Taking on too much
Opportunities	Threats
• Preparing well for supervision so weaknesses can be expressed and worked on • Discussion of cases in supervision, particularly when tempted to solve the client's problems • Applying for training in time management • Observing his own language for signs of sympathy	• Becoming overloaded • Lack of preparation time for supervision • Taking work home on a regular basis • Not being able to 'switch off' from work when he gets home

(continued)

(continued)

Barriers	Aspirations
• Some lack of confidence in his abilities • His view of the world which is different from that of his clients • Lack of time for reflection	• To be known as an outstanding counsellor • To help clients to see their own potential • To enable clients to lead full and satisfying lives
Interests	Needs
• Supporting people • Seeing people overcome their challenges and obstacles • Being there for clients who are struggling	• Making time for reflection • A sounding board for his ideas • Reading literature on time management

---

Reflective activity 2.3

Now spend some time doing a SWOT/B and SWAIN analysis. What does this tell you about yourself that you did not know before?

Motivation

An important aspect of self-awareness is to understand what motivates us. Motivation is a difficult concept to define but includes the processes or factors that prompt us to act in certain ways. This can involve the identification of a particular need and how this might be satisfied, and sometimes involves the process of setting goals. There are many theories that seek to explain what motivation is and how people are motivated, and they can be grouped into two main types: content theories and process theories. In addition, many theories of motivation identify factors that motivate people; some of these factors are external (extrinsic) and some are internal (intrinsic).

Content theories of motivation

Content theories seek to explain what motivation is and the following are the most well known examples of these.

Maslow's hierarchy of needs

Often depicted as a pyramid, Maslow's (1954) hierarchy of needs has the following five levels:

1   Biological and physiological – the need for food, warmth, shelter and sleep.
2   Safety – the need for protection and security.
3   Love and belongingness – the need to feel accepted and loved by others (for example family and friends).

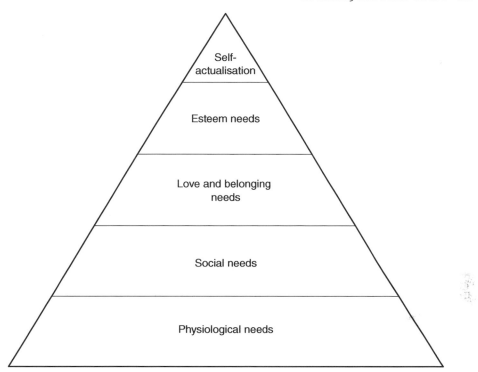

Figure 2.1 Maslow's hierarchy of needs

4   Esteem - the need for achievement, independence, self respect and respect from others.
5   Self-actualisation - the need to realise one's personal potential, self-fulfilment and personal growth.

Maslow's hierarchy is shown in Figure 2.1.

Maslow's work has been heavily criticised, in particular his argument that the needs at the base of the pyramid need to be satisfied before those at a higher level can be achieved. The idea of a 'starving artist', someone who sets all their other needs aside because of their deep desire to self-actualise, seems to be a case in point. However, many professionals who work with homeless people say that their clients find it difficult to think of anything else if they do not know where they will sleep that night.

McGregor's X and Y theory

McGregor's (1970) X and Y theory was developed from the work of Maslow and argues that there are two basic suppositions about people and what motivates them. Type X are people who are motivated by their biological and safety needs towards the bottom of Maslow's hierarchy. They are motivated primarily by extrinsic factors. Type Y are people who are motivated by the top three levels of Maslow's hierarchy and are motivated by extrinsic factors (such as rewards) and intrinsic ones too like a sense of fulfilment. Whether people can be seen in this simple way is, of course, open to debate and many people will only be well motivated when a range of their needs are being met.

Herzberg et al.'s two-factor theory

Herzberg et al. (1959) argued that satisfaction and dissatisfaction were two distinct phenomena associated with motivation caused by two different factors. In their research with engineers and accountants, they found that aspects of the job itself caused satisfaction at work; Herzberg called these factors 'motivators'. By contrast, dissatisfaction was caused by the working environment: the 'hygiene' factors. Some examples of each of the factors are as follows.

Motivators (concerned with the job itself)

- Achievement.
- Recognition.
- The work itself.
- Responsibility.
- Promotion.

Hygiene factors (concerned with the working environment)

- Policy.
- Working conditions.
- Pay.
- Status.
- Job security.

Here, it is possible to see a mixture of extrinsic and intrinsic factors in the motivators and the hygiene factors. This work has also been criticised because of the overlapping nature of the factors; what one person describes as a motivator might be described by another as a hygiene factor.

Process theories of motivation

Process theories seek to explain how people are motivated and here are the most well known examples.

Vroom's expectancy theory

In his expectancy theory, Vroom (1964) argues that people make rational, calculated choices based on the rewards they expect to receive. People value different outcomes and will put effort into activities in proportion to their estimate of the likelihood of achieving what they want. In other words, people will put a lot of effort into something if they feel their chances of success are high and vice versa.

Goal theory

Goal setting has been very influential in many different professional areas and Locke and Latham's (1969) work argues that if we set ourselves challenging goals, we will work hard

Set new goal

Achieve a goal

Set a goal

Figure 2.2 Goal theory

to achieve them. Once we have achieved the goals, we are then in a good position to set some more. This cycle, sometimes called the high performance cycle, is often depicted as an upward moving spiral, as shown in Figure 2.2.

One key aspect is that any goal must be challenging; if the goals we set are too easy to achieve our motivation will probably dwindle. If a goal is not achieved, the result could be a downward spiral.

Equity theory

Equity theory (Adams, 1965) focuses on fairness and argues that people are motivated when they feel they are being treated in an equitable way in relation to their work colleagues. By contrast, people feel de-motivated if they feel they are being required to do more than their colleagues. In general terms, we are happy to put effort into something if we feel that the balance between our output compared to our input is in the same ratio as that of others around us. However, if others put in less and seem to receive more, we feel this is unfair and it de-motivates us.

More recent work (Pink, 2009) proposes that motivation is made up of three key elements and that neglecting these can lead to a lack of motivation.

- Autonomy – most of us like to have some control over our own work. As professionals this is also what we would expect.
- Mastery – the possibility of working at something in order to get better at it.
- Purpose – the opportunity to connect with a larger mission.

Pink argues that the 'carrot and stick' approach to motivation is no longer applicable in a world where people are expected to be creative. Neglecting the three characteristics above and focusing only on goals and outputs means limiting what people can achieve.

Reflective activity 2.4

Now think about what motivates you. Which theory or theories do you find the most helpful in describing your motivation for your work?

Case study 2.4

Sandra is a social worker supporting children and young people with disabilities. Most of the time Sandra enjoys her work and thrives on the challenges it brings. She finds the work itself satisfying, but sometimes gets frustrated by the culture of her organisation. In particular, she finds that people rely on her too much and ask her to do things when they should be asking someone else. This means that Sandra becomes overloaded whilst others seem to have less to do than she does. Sandra decides to ask for support in her next supervision session. She explains the sense of unfairness that she feels and her manager asks her to make a note of when this happens so that it can be addressed.

Transactional Analysis drivers

In Transactional Analysis (TA), recognising our drivers and the ways in which they influence our work and lives is extremely helpful, particularly in relation to motivation. An understanding of TA helps us to identify the origins of our actions and reactions; this means we can then be in a position to change them if we wish. From an examination of Berne's (1964) work, Kahler (1975) defined drivers, which can be seen in the following way.

In Berne's ego state model (Parent Adult Child, often abbreviated to PAC), messages from our parent's or carer's Parent ego state are transacted with and received by our Parent ego state. These are the messages that communicate commands about what to do and what not to do, how we should behave and how we should not. They also lead us to define people and the world, for example 'good people are . . .' and 'bad people are . . .'. These messages are grouped together to make five drivers, which become powerful tools and have a big influence on how we live our lives. Understanding our drivers is vital when thinking about what motivates us.

The five TA drivers are shown below. Each driver has strengths and weaknesses associated with it; like learning styles, weaknesses often emerge when our strengths are overdone. Here are some examples.

- Be Perfect – accurate, eye for detail, neat and tidy but will have a tendency to be harsh on themselves and 'beat themselves up' when they fail to meet their own high standards. They can be harsh on other people too.

- Be Strong - excellent in a crisis, reliable and dependable, makes people feel safe and secure, but does not tend to show their feelings because they do not want to appear weak. This means they may come across as aloof or cold and dis-interested.
- Try Hard - has a very strong work ethic, is persistent and resilient, but sometimes does not know when to stop if something is too difficult. They are often not comfortable when receiving praise.
- Please (people) - great team members who get on well with lots of people. But they never want to upset people and so can be unassertive and often want to rescue people.
- Hurry Up - enthusiastic, achieve a lot in a short space of time, but can be prone to make mistakes because of rushing and lack of forethought.

Recognising our own TA drivers makes us more self-aware. Like learning styles, we can then use our drivers to our advantage, making sure that we do not overdo them, thereby allowing them to become weaknesses. In addition, a knowledge of drivers can help us become more aware of how others are behaving and communicating.

Case study 2.5

Brenda is training to be a mental health nurse and is becoming more self-aware as she is progressing. In particular, she is aware of her strong Please (people) driver; this is a strength in her work as it means that she works very well in a team and is genuinely interested in people, and it makes her compassionate in her work. But she realises that it also has its drawbacks. At times she worries about upsetting people (both colleagues and patients) and this makes her anxious and passive. Brenda's mentor has recognised this and, as a first step, has asked her to observe instances when patients have had to receive difficult information. She would like to discuss these the next time they meet and for Brenda to highlight the strengths and weaknesses in the approaches taken by the staff concerned. Brenda knows that this will help her to consider how she might approach such tasks in the future, using the strengths of her Please (people) driver without succumbing to its weaknesses.

Conclusion

The focus of this chapter has been on becoming more self-aware, which is key to becoming more reflective in your work. We started by examining the concept of the metaphorical mirror by looking at the different kinds of mirrors we use and what these tell us about different aspects of reflective practice. We then moved on to explore learning styles and began to look at how we learn best. This was followed by a SWOT/B and SWAIN analysis. The chapter concluded with an examination of a number of theories of motivation and the concept of TA drivers. All of these different aspects help us to understand ourselves better, which is vital for our professional development. In the next chapter we look at the role of writing in reflection.

References

Adams, J.S. (1965) 'Inequality is social exchange' in L. Berkowitz (ed.) *Advances in Experimental Psychology*, 2, New York: Academic Press.

Berne, E. (1964) *Games People Play*, London: Penguin Books.

Herzberg, F., Mausner, B. and Synderman, B.B. (1959) *The Motivation to Work*, New York: John Wiley.

Honey, P. and Mumford, A. (2000) *The Learning Styles Helper's Guide*, Maidenhead: Peter Honey Publications.

Kahler, T. (1975). 'Drivers: The Key to the Process Scripts'. *Transactional Analysis Journal*, 5(3): 280-4.

Kolb, D. (1984) *Experiential Learning: Experience as the Source of Learning and Development*, Upper Saddle River, NJ: Prentice Hall.

Locke, E.A. and Latham, G.P. (1990) 'Work and motivation: the high performance cycle', in U. Kleinbeck, H-H. Quast and H. Hacker (eds) *Work Motivation*, Brighton: Lawrence Erlbaum Associates.

Maslow, A.H. (1954) *Motivation and Personality*, New York: Harper and Row.

McGregor, G. (1970) *The Human Side of Enterprise*, Maidenhead: McGraw-Hill.

Merton, T. (1971) *Contemplation in a World of Action*, New York: Garden City, pp. 178-9.

Osterman, K.F. and Kottkamp, R.B. (2004) *Reflective Practice for Educators*, 2nd edn Thousand Oaks, CA: Corwin Press.

Pink, D. (2009) *Drive: The Surprising Truth about What Motivates Us*, New York: Riverhead Books.

Schön, D.A. (1983) *The Reflective Practitioner*, Aldershot: Ashgate.

Vroom, V.H. (1964) *Work and Motivation*, New York: John Wiley.

Williams, M. and Penman, D. (2011) *Mindfulness: A Practical Guide to Finding Peace in a Frantic World*, London: Piatkus.

3 The role of writing in reflection

'Writing to me is simply thinking through my fingers.'

(Isaac Asimov, personal communication)

Introduction

Many writers on the subject of reflection suggest writing as one key way of engaging in the reflective process. In this chapter we discuss how writing can help us to reflect at a deeper level and we look at some tools that can enable us to do this more easily and effectively. In particular, the use of a reflective diary or journal will be highlighted. The chapter concludes with suggestions of other ways to engage in reflection at a deeper level.

Why writing?

So why is writing thought to be important in the area of reflection? There is no doubt that writing in itself is a skilful activity. In primary schools the development of the writing skills of most young children lags behind that of their reading skills. When we were young we probably learned to read more quickly than we learned to write. As a whole, writing is a much more difficult skill to master, hence on any programme of study the most difficult tasks are likely to be the written assignments.

So what makes writing difficult? In the early days of my role as a university lecturer I attended a writers' seminar with a professor whom I respected and admired. Something he said that day seemed very significant to me and stayed in my memory – his words were 'I write about something in order to understand it'. He was clearly very knowledgeable in relation to his field of study and I had always assumed that he wrote a lot (papers, books etc.) because he understood a lot. In fact, the opposite was the case; it was the process of writing that helped him to understand things.

This is an important point in relation to reflective writing – if you want to understand more about yourself and your practice, you need to write about it. It is almost impossible to write something whilst talking about something else, unless you are writing and speaking things that you know 'off by heart' (e.g. writing your address whilst reciting a nursery rhyme), and even then it is very difficult to do – I have tried, and so have some of my students! The act of putting pen to paper involves thinking about what you are writing, making decisions about what to write, how to write it, processing your thoughts and explaining what you mean so that, if appropriate, someone else can read it and understand what you have written. Put simply, the act of writing helps us to develop our understanding.

Neuroscience shows us that writing as an activity stimulates the reticular activating system (RAS) at the base of the brain. The RAS acts as a filter for everything our brain needs to process, making sure that we give more importance to what we are actively focusing on at that moment. The act of writing, therefore, enables us to sharpen our focus and will often be a much more effective way of learning something than, for example, discussion. As a result, you will be much more likely to remember what you have written down (there is a good lesson here in relation to taking notes in lectures and seminars) than what you have discussed. And, of course, it gives you a record of your learning that you can go back to.

Moon (2006) identifies some of the aims of reflective diary writing as part of the process of professional learning and development. They are as follows.

- To record experience. Often you think you will remember, but you don't, particularly at times when you are trying to 'take a lot in'.
- To facilitate learning from experience. It helps you to examine your experiences in some depth.
- To support understanding and how this is then represented. It helps you to understand things and to then be able to discuss them or write about them when being assessed.
- To help you develop critical thinking and a questioning attitude. It prevents you from accepting things 'at face value'.
- It increases metacognition, or thinking about thinking.
- It increases active involvement in learning and the ownership of it.
- It increases thinking skills.
- It enhances problem solving skills.
- It can be used as a form of assessment.
- It enhances the process of reflective practice, enabling you to think at a deeper level.
- It enhances personal development and self-empowerment.
- It is therapeutic.
- It enhances creativity.
- It develops the skills of writing.
- It is a form of self-expression.
- It supports planning and achievement in projects.
- It serves as a means of communication when shared, for example, with a fellow student, tutor or mentor.

But is writing something by hand the same as typing it on a computer keyboard? This is less clear. Recent research with students (Mueller and Oppenheimer, 2014) suggests that it is not, and shows that they understand more when writing by hand than when using a keyboard. Of course each of us has our own particular preferences – some of us like a nice notebook and pen, others like a laptop, tablet or smart phone. Two things are worth noting: first, when we get to the point where we can type more quickly than we can write, writing then slows us down and gives us more thinking time; in our hectic lives this can be very valuable. Second, it is easier to delete words and phrases when using a keyboard than when writing by hand. This might result in us being too selective about what we write; there is always a temptation to write what we think we should write, rather than what we want to write.

Here are four important messages in relation to reflective writing: the first is to 'write' and not to procrastinate. It is very easy to think we will remember things, particularly significant things, but in reality, when life is so busy, we probably won't. We might be tempted to think 'a lot has happened today, I'll write about it later' and events simply overtake us and we then forget even very significant things that we thought we would always remember. The second is to do what suits you best. It can be a mistake to waste time thinking about how to record things. Those with a strong Reflector style (Honey and Mumford, 2000) can easily slip into thinking so much about the kind of notebook to buy, the very best pen, whether to use a laptop or not and so on that they fail to start writing – I know this to my peril! The third is to be realistic. Reflective writing does not need to be 'perfect' and, indeed, it should not be so; it needs to be manageable. In my experience, an individual can achieve a lot by devoting as little as 15 minutes a week to this type of writing. The fourth is to be practical and not to be hard on yourself. Suffice it to say that it is possible that I might have written a better book if I had written it all by hand first, but this was not something I felt I could contemplate!

Reflective activity 3.1

Now think about what is stopping you from starting to write reflectively. If you have started this process already, how are you getting on? What are you enjoying and what is difficult? Now write some notes.

Case study 3.1

Gloria has recently started a course in social work and is being encouraged by her tutors to write some reflections on her learning. She has never done this kind of writing before, but feels she would like to try to capture some of the many things she feels she is learning. She usually uses a laptop when taking notes, so tries using this for her reflections. Whilst she finds this useful, she is always tempted to delete what she has typed as she feels it is never good enough. Some of her fellow students are writing by hand instead and many of them seem to enjoy it and to find it therapeutic as a means of processing their learning experiences. Gloria decides to try writing this way, but finds it a much slower process. She decides to use her laptop when she feels she hasn't much time and wants to be sure not to forget things and to write by hand when she has more time. This seems to work well for Gloria and she is pleased to have found a balance that she can work with.

What is reflective writing?

If you are studying on a professional programme, it is likely that you will be asked to write reflectively, so it is important to understand what this means. It is also helpful to understand what it is not. So what do we mean by the term reflective writing?

Reflective writing is always written in the first person. For those who have been used to studying for a while, this will be unusual. Most academic writing is done in the third person (he/she, it, one etc.), but those who write reflectively use the language of I, me, we and us, which makes it more personal than most other forms of academic writing. Bearing in mind that reflective practice demands a high level of self-awareness and writing plays is a key part in helping us to develop this, it should come as no surprise that writing reflectively demands that we write about ourselves.

Reflective writing is critical in nature. As a term, it is important to understand what the word critical means. The first thing that might spring to your mind when you hear the word critical is negative, but this can take you down a dangerous path where you see only the negative things about yourself and your practice. The word critique is more accurate here as reflective writing asks you to evaluate your work. For example, a restaurant critic will offer a critique of their dining experience, focusing on what was good as well as what could be improved, assuming they enjoyed at least some of their food anyway! This means that reflective writing is not descriptive; it is more than simply writing down what happened.

In my experience, some students can struggle with understanding how to write analytically and might receive feedback with comments such as 'too descriptive' and 'more analysis needed'. Here, the idea of a SWOT analysis (see Chapter 2) is helpful with its emphasis on strengths and weaknesses. Writing about these will make your work more analytical. However, reflective writing also involves considering your thoughts, engaging with your emotions (see Chapter 6) and challenging your assumptions (see Chapter 7). In relation to

Table 3.1 Reflective writing

Reflective writing is:	Reflective writing is not:
Written in the first person (I, me, we, us)	Written in the third person (he, she, it, they)
Critical in the sense of offering a critique	Critical in the sense of only focusing on the negative
Analytical	Descriptive
Spontaneous	Calculated
Free flowing	'Doctored', what I think I should write
Honest	'Kidding myself'
Subjective	Objective
About engaging with my feelings and processing them	A means of ignoring my feelings and burying them
A tool for helping me to challenge my assumptions	An excuse to ignore my assumptions and allow them to influence my work in a negative way
An investment of time	A waste of time

diaries and journals, reflective writing is honest and spontaneous. This kind of writing is considered in the final section of this chapter. There is no doubt that reflective writing takes time, but many students who engage with it find that it is time well spent.

Table 3.1 summarises what reflective writing is and what it is not.

How to start writing reflectively

Whether you are writing an essay, a speech or a book, one of the most difficult aspects is where to start. If you are being asked to write reflectively you may well feel that you do not know where to begin. In my experience, students often pose questions such as 'So, what am I meant to write?', 'How do I start?' and 'What if my writing makes no sense?' The simplest way is just to start writing, and Stage 1 of Bolton's (2014: 136) exercise entitled the Six Minute Write offers these very useful pointers.

- This is a timed exercise, so time yourself and write for six minutes without stopping.
- Write whatever comes to mind and let your writing flow freely.
- Keep writing and do not pause to think too much about what you are writing.
- Do not pause to analyse what you have written, otherwise you will be tempted to write what you think you should write rather than what you want to write.
- Keep writing even if it does not make much sense to you.
- Do not worry about spelling, punctuation, grammar or jargon.
- Allow yourself to write anything.
- This is your writing and whatever you write is correct because it is yours.
- Remember, no-one else needs to read what you have written.
- Stop after six minutes and look at how much you have been able to write.

Reflective activity 3.2

Now try Bolton's Six Minute Write. Remember to time yourself. Then think about this experience of writing and write some notes on how you got on. Was it easier or more difficult than you thought?

Case study 3.2

Peter has just started a course to train to be a counsellor and his tutor is asking every student to reflect on their learning and the development of their interpersonal skills. Peter is unsure where to start as reflective writing is a new thing for him, so he decides to try the Six Minute Write; this is what he wrote when he tried it.

Well, I've never written anything like this before! When I wrote at school I was always told to be really careful - make sure your spelling and grammar are correct, don't use abbreviations, make it sound formal. This is totally different! Feels

(continued)

(continued)

> quite liberating! But, is it any good? Is this the kind of thing the tutor means? I guess I'll find out at some point. The tutor says 'Just write what's in your head' so here goes. Today we did our first role play exercises and how scary was that? I always knew that the course would involve this and I do enjoy talking with people, but trying out listening skills and asking open questions is all really difficult. I felt so nervous and forgot what to do. The people I was working with seemed so much better than me – I know I've got so much to learn it's frightening. Will I ever be able to do this? I really don't know, but I do know I'm going to try.

As with Peter, the Six Minute Write should help you to get started. Bolton also puts forward four other stages of reflective writing that you can try, and she suggests other forms that it might take. Stage 2 involves thinking of an experience that you have had and writing about it as if you are telling a story. In Stage 3 you can then read the story (and the six minutes of writing) and respond to it. In Stage 4 she suggests sharing what you have written with someone else – this needs to be someone you know well and trust (see Chapter 8). In Stage 5 she suggests you could begin to develop your work by writing from someone else's perspective, for example from the client's point of view.

A structure for reflective writing

If you are new to reflective writing you might find it helpful to have a structure for your writing. This can help you to make a start, and you might then discard it later as your experience in this area grows. Knott and Scragg (2013) offer a very useful structure for writing a reflective journal, which can be helpful for people who are unsure about what to write. This structure is based on three stages, each with useful accompanying questions to encourage reflection at a deeper level.

Stage 1 – Reflecting

Here, the suggestion is that you focus on an issue or a concern that you have in relation to your practice and development. Like Bolton (2014), they advise you to write freely and spontaneously in order to capture your thoughts and feelings.

Stage 2 – Analyse

This is the most complex of the stages and involves responding to the following key questions:

- What is happening?
- What assumptions am I making?
- What does all of this show about my underlying beliefs?
- Are there alternative ways of looking at this, if so what are they? (e.g. from the perspective of someone else – a colleague, the client, a manager). This particular aspect is similar to Bolton's (2014) Stage 5.

Stage 3 – Action

The focus here is on the action you could take following the analysis. Again, the authors suggest considering some key questions:

- What action could I take?
- How can I learn from this experience?
- How might I respond if this situation occurred again?
- What can I learn from this experience regarding my beliefs about myself?

Reflective activity 3.3

Now try using Knott and Scragg's structure to reflect on something that has happened this week. How helpful was it?

Case study 3.3

Ella is training as a teacher in early years and wants to develop her reflective writing skills. She decides to use Knott and Scragg's structure for reflective writing, and here is an example of what she wrote after a particularly difficult day.

Stage 1 – had a really tricky day today in the nursery. Some of the children seemed to be really difficult and at times it felt like it was all getting on top of me. In particular one little girl seemed to be snatching toys from the other children. Usually I cope well with this, but today I thought I might lose my temper with her. Usually I love my work, and I had designed such a good activity for them, but they just didn't seem interested. I couldn't wait till the end of the day. I just wanted to go home and collapse in a heap. Tomorrow will be another day and hopefully it will be better than today – otherwise I think I might give up.

Stage 2 – so what's going on? I know I love being with children and love the work – so why did it go so badly today? I thought the activity I had planned was really good. But maybe it was too much and too difficult – I think I was really disappointed because I'd put such a lot of work into it. I did spend most of last night preparing it. Maybe the timing wasn't good? Maybe they were just tired? Or maybe I didn't explain it properly. Or was it just boring? I know I was tired too, which doesn't help.

Stage 3 I think I need to talk to my mentor about what happened. I feel a failure, but need to remember that the children are very young and can only concentrate for so long. I also need to think about the time of day for doing bigger activities. Maybe it would have been better earlier in the day when the children have more energy and can concentrate for longer. I need to be sure to get a good night's sleep. Maybe I have more energy earlier in the day too – I will definitely talk to my mentor.

Knott and Scragg also suggest looking back over a number of diary entries to see if there are any key themes emerging over time. This can help you to highlight some specific areas you would like to work on.

Using a structure such as this means that your reflective writing will move from mere description of what happened to analysis and evaluation. You will no doubt begin to gain significant insights into yourself and your practice as you document your personal and professional development.

Using a reflective diary or journal to aid professional growth

Many students on professional courses are encouraged to keep a reflective log, diary or journal to aid their professional development. We have already established the role that writing can play in relation to learning, but why is writing regularly seen to be important? First, we need to distinguish the difference between a log, a diary and a journal.

> A log tends to suggest describing things that happen, such as logging events. When hearing the word log, some of you might remember the 'Captain's log, stardate . . .' where the voyages of the Starship Enterprise were recorded. The purpose of this, like most other logs, is to record what happened. Imagine being a crew member and trying to remember all the different events and galaxies visited – without the aid of a log this would be impossible!
>
> A diary implies regular writing (daily, weekly) and offers some kind of structure, perhaps with spaces to write at regular intervals. Many of us also use diaries to help us to remember dates and times, to plan ahead and to prioritise our work and lives. Losing a diary can make us panic, whether we leave a paper version on the bus or forget to back up our laptop, hence the growth in automated updating systems online. A diary provides a dated record so we can see what happened and when.
>
> A journal is most often a nice quality notebook filled with blank pages. People who enjoy writing might buy a travel journal for a particular period or holiday. It might have a nice cover with a picture of the globe on the outside, but most of the pages inside will be blank, encouraging people to write freely about their experiences. A journal is viewed as a personal item, so what someone buys to use as a journal is an individual choice and will vary greatly; journal enthusiasts may even buy a notebook and decorate the cover themselves. A journal tends to provide a more detailed record of a period of time and is something that can be read in the future to bring back memories of a specific period of time.

In some respects the terminology used to describe what you write in is irrelevant and the quality of what you write is much more important. People who are new to reflective writing might start with a log and move to the more structured form of a diary later as their confidence grows. Others will enjoy the structure of a diary and move on later to a free flowing journal format. Experienced journal writers may start with a blank notebook, but for those who are new to reflective writing this can be a scary prospect.

Engaging in reflective writing is a process and, as well as using something like Bolton's exercise to help you to get started, it is also well worth considering how you can keep yourself motivated to continue writing. Bassot's (2013) journal is written for students on professional courses and, as well as providing space to write, it also contains content on a range of topics related to reflective practice; it could be a valuable tool for some. Simple motivational strategies to try to ensure that you find writing enjoyable are important, such as having a nice pen or background and font to use on your tablet.

Case study 3.4

Leroy is training to be a physiotherapist and is facing a challenging placement working with patients who have suffered from spinal injuries. Leroy used to enjoy reflective writing when he began his studies, but now finds that he doesn't have the time to give to it that he feels he should. Leroy is anxious about his placement as he knows that he will probably face some very demanding situations with patients who have major injuries. He feels that he needs to slow down and take some time to reflect at regular intervals. Leroy decides to 'kick start' his reflections by buying a small high quality notebook for his reflections. He chooses one that will fit into his pocket at work, so that he can carry it round with him and note things down in it during his breaks. He also decides to write in his notebook for ten minutes at the end of each shift to capture his thoughts. Leroy soon finds that he enjoys writing again and can see that he is processing his professional learning in a more thorough way than he has in the past.

Is it all about writing?

We have established how writing helps us to develop our understanding in all sorts of different areas, but are there other useful ways of doing this too? There is no doubt that technology can play a part in this, particularly if you are a person who loves your laptop, smart phone or tablet like I do. Many of us have now reached the point where we feel bereft if we forget our mobile phone and use laptops or tablets to organise our work and lives. The beauty of being able to 'back up' everything calms our fears of losing important data should we no longer have our favourite gadget.

So how can we harness such things to advance our reflective skills? Here are some ideas:

- Send yourself a text message or email describing your day, outlining what was enjoyable and difficult about it and then read it.
- Set an alarm on your smart phone to remind you to reflect on significant events on particular days.
- Use your online calendar to give yourself a regular reminder to spend some time reflecting (e.g. weekly).
- Make an arrangement with your critical friend (see Chapter 8) to send a text message at certain times to encourage you to spend some time reflecting, or simply to find out how you are getting on.

For those of you who love all things artistic there are other ways of reflecting by using your artistic flair to help you to reflect. This could include:

- Drawing.
- Painting.
- Collage.
- Model making.
- A range of crafts such as sewing, tapestry, quilting.

For those of us who feel this kind of thing is not for us, don't forget that techniques such as some simple diagrams or mind maps can also work well to help us to illustrate our thoughts.

Reflective activity 3.4

Think of some other resources you can use to help you to reflect. Now write some notes on how and when you could use these.

Case study 3.5

Jane is working in a further education college with students who are speakers of other languages. She wants to encourage them to think about their learning experiences from the past as she feels this will help them to move forward in their studies, but she knows that for some of them, being able to articulate abstract thoughts in English is very difficult. In a tutorial session Jane decides to ask the students to reflect on their learning by using collage. She brings in a pile of old magazines, flip chart paper, scissors and glue and asks the students to choose pictures that represent their education so far. As they are working, she asks the students to write down a few thoughts on what each picture represents. The students enjoy the activity and Jane is surprised that those students who usually find it very difficult to share their thoughts are able to read what they have written in a relatively easy way. Jane joins in the activity too and is reminded of how she feels about her own learning and development. She chooses the following pictures – a clock to remind her of her desire to make time for reflection, a family group to illustrate the support she has from home and a jigsaw puzzle to remind her of the many and varied aspects of her professional knowledge and skills that she is seeking to develop.

Conclusion

In this chapter we have considered a range of issues in the whole area of reflective writing. It is clear that writing helps us to reflect at a deeper level, and some aids have been introduced that should help you to write more reflectively. A useful structure has been presented to help you to get started, whilst encouraging you to use a reflective diary or journal for your professional growth. The chapter concluded with ideas for using other resources to help you to reflect. In the next chapter we move on to the whole area of learning from experience.

References

Bassot, B. (2013) *The Reflective Journal*, Basingstoke: Palgrave Macmillan.
Bolton, G. (2014) *Reflective Practice: Writing and Professional Development*, 4th edn, London: Sage.
Honey, P. and Mumford, A. (2000) *The Learning Styles Helper's Guide*, Maidenhead: Peter Honey Publications.
Knott, C. and Scragg, T. (2013) *Reflective Practice in Social Work*, 3rd edn., London: Learning Matters.
Moon, J. (2006) *Learning Journals: A Handbook for Reflective Practice and Professional Development*, 2nd edn., Abingdon: Routledge.
Mueller, P.A. and Oppenheimer, D.M. (2014) 'The pen is mightier than the keyboard: advantages of longhand over laptop note taking', *Psychological Science*, 25: 1159-68.

4 Experiential learning

'One must learn by doing the thing; for though you think you know it you have no certainty, until you try.'

(Sophocles)

Introduction

Programmes of professional education and training, such as teaching, nursing, social work and counselling typically include periods of time spent on placement or in a workplace. Many students speak of these times as being particularly significant in their learning. In the same way as it would be impossible to learn how to drive without getting behind the wheel of a car, becoming a competent practitioner in these areas would seem impossible without some 'hands on' experience. It is generally accepted therefore, that learning from experience plays a vital part in professional training and development. In this chapter we examine what learning from experience means and we look at some key theoretical approaches that explain how we learn in this way. In addition, we consider why we do not always learn from experience and how we can address areas of non-learning.

What do we mean by learning from experience?

Most people learn from experience throughout their everyday lives. For example, phrases such as 'that worked well' or, conversely, 'I won't make that mistake again' show that often (but not always) people take note of what happens around them and take action on it as a result. In addition to this informal learning from experience, students on professional programmes have structured times of placement or work experience to help them to become skilled and knowledgeable in their chosen area of professional practice.

Many writers on the subject of experiential learning use cycles to describe how we learn, and in this chapter we critically examine three particular models that have become popular in this area. These models help us to understand how we can maximise our learning to develop and improve our professional practice.

The ERA cycle

The ERA cycle summarises three of the main components of reflective practice (Jasper, 2013). The first is Experience, or the things that happen to us. The second is the Reflective processes that help us to think through the experiences we have had; these processes help us to learn from our experiences. And the third is Action, which follows as a result of our reflections. The ERA model is often shown as a triangle with Experience at the top, Reflection at the bottom right and Action at the bottom left. Arrows on the triangle suggest that Experience is followed by Reflection, which in turn is followed by Action.

Kolb's experiential learning cycle

From his background as a psychologist and his interest in organisational behaviour, Kolb developed his experiential learning cycle; his work has become seminal in this area. Kolb was interested in how people learn at work and how they make sense of their experiences in organisations. Heavily influenced by the work of Kurt Lewin, Kolb (1984) developed his experiential learning cycle to depict how people learn from experience. The model is depicted below in Figure 4.1.

The diagram shows that there are four stages in the cycle that are depicted as following on from each other in sequence. Kolb argues that the cycle can begin at any point; however, often, but not always, the cycle starts with a Concrete Experience. This can be something fairly mundane or something new or strikingly different from what we would usually expect.

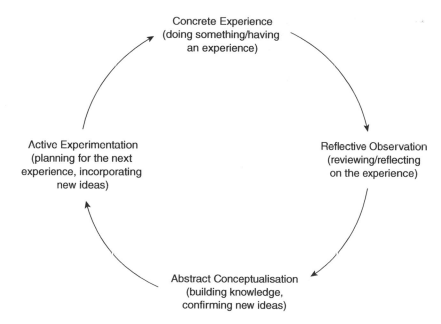

Figure 4.1 Kolb's experiential learning cycle

Following the experience, the next stage is Reflective Observation where we think about what has occurred and begin to analyse it. This is then followed by the third stage on the cycle called Abstract Conceptualisation where we start to generalise from what we have experienced, adding to our knowledge of certain situations and practices. In the final stage, Active Experimentation, we are able to begin to apply the knowledge we have acquired to new situations and the next experience; the cycle (or spiral as it is sometimes depicted) then starts again. The experiential learning process could happen in a period of moments, days, weeks or months depending on the situation.

Reflective activity 4.1

Now write some notes about an experience you have had recently where you feel you have learned a lot. How can you apply the stages of Kolb's cycle to this?

Case study 4.1

Cheryl is studying for a BEd in Primary Education and is doing her final placement with a class of pupils in Year 6. She has enjoyed her previous placements; she feels that her confidence is growing and she now wants to make the most of her remaining time as a student in order to learn as much as she can before she starts work as a newly qualified teacher. Cheryl knows that she has a strong Activist learning style, which has been a real strength in the classroom. She works hard and achieves a lot with the pupils. However, she does not always find reflection easy and her mentor has asked her to work on this, as she feels it will help Cheryl to become a good all round teacher. Cheryl decides to try using Kolb's cycle to give her reflections some structure. She uses her lesson plan to remind her of an experience and annotates it in order to reflect on how the session went. From this, Cheryl is able to identify things that went well and those aspects of the lesson that she feels could be improved. On the back of the lesson plan, Cheryl writes notes under the headings of Abstract Conceptualisation and Active Experimentation to record the new knowledge she has gained through the experience and ideas that she can use when planning a similar exercise in the future. She discusses this with her mentor, who suggests that Cheryl could do this kind of activity with the pupils too as part of their preparation for transferring to secondary school.

When considering Kolb's cycle it is important to remember that it is just one explanation of how we learn from experience and, like any other model, it is important to critique it. The arrows on the cycle point in one direction only, which implies that one stage follows neatly after another; in practice this is unlikely to happen each time we learn. While Kolb argues that the cycle often starts with the Concrete Experience, our learning styles (Honey and Mumford, 2000, see Chapter 2) could also play a key part in where we begin on the cycle. Examples are given in Figures 4.2–4.6.

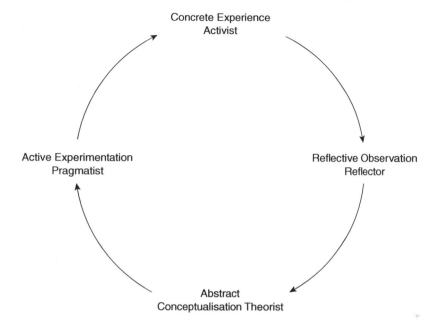

Figure 4.2 Kolb's experiential learning cycle and Honey and Mumford's learning styles

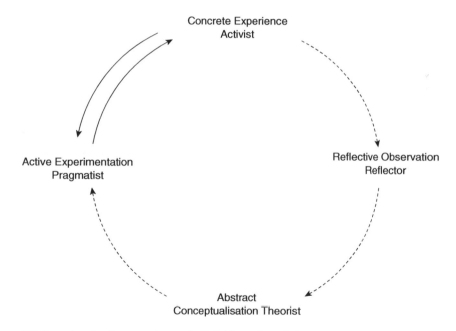

Figure 4.3 People who have a strong Activist learning style

Those who have a strong Activist learning style will often want to act quickly and are likely to start the cycle with a Concrete Experience. Some will skip the next two stages and immediately want to prepare to 'have another go'.

Those who are Reflectors will feel much happier having thought things through first and might 'dip their toes into the water' of the experience only following some detailed planning.

Theorists will often want to go to the library first to read up on relevant details and models and will look at how they apply to the experience. They may be unhappy if they cannot see how their preferred theory works in practice and then go back to the library to read some more.

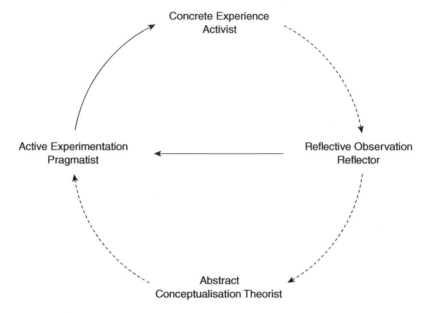

Figure 4.4 People who have a strong Reflector learning style

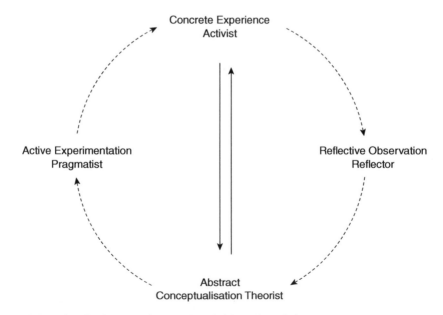

Figure 4.5 People who have a strong Theorist learning style

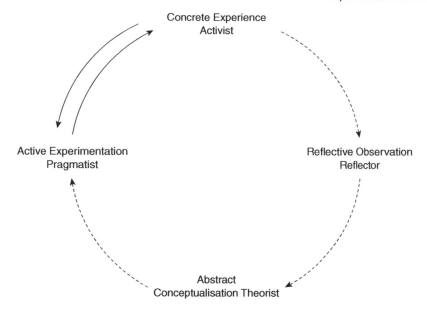

Figure 4.6 People who have a strong Pragmatist learning style

Pragmatists may well want to plan before they act and if things do not go as expected, they might be tempted to do more planning.

All of this means that, in practice, individuals can begin the cycle at any point and travel round the cycle in numerous different directions. In their Learning Styles Handbook, Honey and Mumford examine a large number of possibilities in this regard; this is far removed from Kolb's unidirectional cycle. However, one of Kolb's arguments seems clear; in order to learn most from experience, we need to engage with each stage on the cycle. Missing stages altogether (as in all the examples above) by focusing too much on our learning style preferences means that we will fail to maximise our learning.

Finally, it is important to remember that any model that argues for a particular sequence of events will always be flawed. It will face the inevitable question 'So, does it always happen like that?' And invariably the answer will be 'probably not'.

Reflective activity 4.2

Now think about your recent experience again. Were there stages on the cycle that you missed and, if so, why do you think that was? Does this link with your learning style preferences?

Reflection-on-action

In Chapter 1 we considered Schön's (1983) concept of reflection-in-action, which formed a central part of his arguments on the need for professional practitioners to adopt a reflective approach. He also wrote in far less detail about what he called reflection-on-action; the kind of thinking that professionals engage in following an experience. This is a reminder of the second stage (Reflective Observation) of Kolb's (1984) cycle.

Reflection-on-action is particularly important for people who work in the minor professions (see page 9), as there is usually no single correct response to any situation we might encounter. Indeed, mistakes can easily be made if we think 'I've come across this kind of situation before. Doing X helped then, so it will probably work now', as invariably it will not. Each case is unique, and this demands creative thinking at a deeper level on the part of practitioners and an openness to working at finding the most appropriate approach for the particular situation. There is simply no 'one size fits all' model or approach that can be applied in every case. Using the metaphor of bespoke tailoring, Thompson (2005: 196) aptly describes reflective practice as 'cutting the cloth to suit the specific circumstances, rather than looking for ready-made solutions'. And reflection-on-action forms a key part of this process as practitioners reflect following an experience to seek what works best for that particular client.

So why is reflection-on-action needed? As professional practitioners we need to resist the temptation to accept things at face value. Reflection-on-action helps us to take an analytical approach to our practice and to consider things from a number of different perspectives. As well as identifying how we can improve and find solutions to problems we might identify, reflection-on-action also helps us to see what went well and to build on that. This in turn helps us to build our professional knowledge through Abstract Conceptualisation (stage 3 on Kolb's cycle) as we think about how we could adapt our practice and approach things next time via Active Experimentation (stage 4 on Kolb's cycle).

Case study 4.2

Neil is training to be a social worker and has always enjoyed reading; he has identified that he has a strong Theorist learning style. He is an analytical person who likes to examine a range of theories to find the best approach to any given situation. Once he has found his preferred approach, he enjoys applying the model and working towards a solution. As he progresses, Neil finds that he has 'tried and tested' methods, which help him to feel confident. But after a while Neil finds that his methods do not always work as well as he expects and he finds this frustrating. When this happens, he is always tempted to try again, but usually with little success. Neil realises that instead of seeking answers in books, he needs to reflect on the experiences he is having, to try and identify what is not working and why. As time progresses, he realises that in many situations he cannot simply apply one approach, but needs to draw on aspects of a number of approaches to support the particular client he is working with at the time.

Reflection-on-action is central to reflective practice as it can prevent stagnation through routine. It demands that we turn off our 'autopilot' and see each situation afresh. However, this does not mean that we need, or indeed will be able, to spend time reflecting on every detail of our professional lives; this would simply be too exhausting. But reflection-on-action means being open to new ideas and through it our practice can develop and remain vibrant.

Driscoll's 'What?' model

People who are new to reflective practice often find a simple, straightforward model useful when seeking to learn from their experiences. In particular, Driscoll's (2007) 'What?' model (drawn from Borton's Developmental Framework, 1970) is an example of such a model. Like Kolb's (1984) model, it is drawn as a cycle (or in this case as a spiral) with arrows pointing clockwise.

The model has the following three steps:

Step 1 – What? – this involves writing a description of an event or an experience.
Step 2 – So what? – here we reflect on the event or experience and start to analyse selected aspects of it.
Step 3 – Now what? – a range of proposed action points are devised following the experience, focusing on what has been learned. When depicted diagrammatically, a number of arrows are drawn from Step 3 to represent a range of possible actions that could be taken in the light of our experience.

Driscoll has also formulated a number of useful trigger questions to help us to use the model effectively, including:

Step 1 – What? – how did I react and what did others do who were involved?
Step 2 – So what? – do I feel troubled in any way, and if so, how?
Step 3 – Now what? – how can I change my approach if I face a similar situation again and what are my main learning points? What different options are there for me?

Case study 4.3

Dan is training to be a nurse in elderly care and wants to reflect on the experiences he is gaining on his placement. Dan decides to use the questions in Driscoll's model to help him to begin to analyse what he is learning.

Step 1 – how did I react to the experience and what did others do who were involved?
Today I was observing an experienced community nurse change a dressing on a man's leg that is badly infected. The man was nervous and became very distressed – he has had dressings replaced regularly and knows that the process is very painful. I felt awful about causing him more pain. The community nurse seemed very calm and spoke to him in a reassuring way. She asked him if he would like some pain relief and he said yes. She sat with him for ten minutes to make sure that the pain relief was working and spoke with him about his grandson's visit that he was looking forward to at the weekend. This definitely seemed to put him at ease.
Step 2 – do I feel troubled in any way, and if so, how? She made it all look so easy. How would I cope if I had to do this? As a nurse I am meant to relieve pain not cause it. She focused on the patient while I focused on myself.

(continued)

(continued)

Step 3 – how can I change my approach if I face a similar situation again and what are my main learning points? What different options are there for me? I learned a lot from the community nurse. She was very caring but firm. She knew the man's dressing needed to be changed but did everything in a very calm and kind way. She distracted him and helped him to relax. These are all strategies that I can try in the future if I have to do this. Nursing isn't only about my clinical skills; my interpersonal skills are vital, as is compassion and understanding for my patients.

Driscoll's model is simple and the three stages – 'What?', 'So What?', 'What next?' – are easy to remember, particularly when you are new to professional practice and it seems like there is so much to learn. In particular, the question 'Do I feel troubled in any way?' is extremely useful as our feelings can act as a prompt to deeper thinking and exploration (see Chapter 6). However, after a while you may find that you want to reflect at a deeper level so, if appropriate, you should feel free to use this in the early days of your practice and then to move on to other approaches. This means that your reflective skills will develop alongside the other key skills that you use in professional practice.

Reflective activity 4.3

Now try using Driscoll's model to reflect on a recent experience. How does it compare to using Kolb's model? Where are the similarities and differences?

Learning as transformation

It is widely accepted that learning has the potential to transform a person's life, and as you progress in your studies and in your professional life you may feel that you are becoming a different person. Looking back on my own professional life, I know that I am not the same as the person who initially trained to be a Careers Adviser.

Illeris (2014), drawing on the work of Taylor (2009), identifies the following six principles that can lead to transformative learning.

1   Acknowledging individual experience – this is the previous experience that each learner brings with them, which forms a starting point for learning. When this is recognised and valued, people are more likely to reflect on their current position and to challenge themselves through experience.
2   Encouraging critical reflection – this involves paying attention to three key elements: the meaning people extract from what they are learning, the process (or how people are learning) and the premises (or the context for learning). The latter appears to be particularly significant for transformative learning to take place.
3   Engaging in discussion and dialogue – a dialogue with self and others is vital as this prompts critical reflection and this is how individuals discover their boundaries.

4   Having a holistic orientation – people need to learn as whole beings. This includes engaging with their emotions (see Chapter 6) and their context. This happens through a process of 'see-feel-change' (Taylor, 2009: 10).

5   Being aware of context – having an appreciation of their context and their experiences – means that people are more likely to adapt to change. In particular, being aware of the time constraints of life and how to manage them is significant for learning as transformative learning takes time.

6   Building authentic relationships – this is a particularly important element for people who are training to be teachers and mentors. It involves being open and honest and allowing learners to question their growing understanding. This enables the person in training to understand themselves and their practice better and allows their confidence to grow.

Reflective activity 4.4

Looking at the six principles above, which do you feel is most important for your professional learning and why?

Overall, Illeris argues that a learner-centred approach is most likely to lead to transformation, and experiences that enable people to develop at their own pace and in ways that are most suited to them are most likely to succeed. However, this presents challenges for students and teachers alike because the syllabus or the National Occupational Standards for the particular sector still needs to be met. The rise of competence frameworks has done much to restrict flexibility in professional training, although the maintenance of standards is vital for the well being of clients and professionals.

Do we always learn from experience?

Whilst it is widely accepted that learning has the potential to transform people's lives (Illeris, 2014), when we look back honestly at our own lives and those of others it becomes clear that this does not always happen. This also applies to learning from experience. As one student who was training to be a Careers Adviser once said to me, 'I don't understand why I keep making the same mistakes. I know what I need to do and when I go into the assessment, it's clear, but when it comes to it, I just don't seem able to do it'. Why is this? If it were as simple as 'practice makes perfect' why is it that in some situations improvement does not happen automatically?

The work of Jarvis (2003) gives us some useful indicators about a range of responses we can have to learning experiences. He views learning as a more complex process and explains that it does not always happen following an experience. Based on the work of Kolb, he carried out research with adult learners to try and identify how learning took place. The cycle he then developed (much more complex than Kolb's cycle) can be traversed via nine different routes depending on how the person responds to an experience. The routes themselves are not specified because of the difficulties of isolating them and because an individual might be able to follow more than one route in any one experience. However, the cycle is described as having the following nine aspects.

1   The person having the experience.
2   The situation.
3   The experience.
4   The person: reinforced but relatively unchanged.
5   Practice experimentation.
6   Memorisation.
7   Reasoning and reflecting.
8   Evaluation.
9   The person: changed and more experienced.

This is depicted in Figure 4.7.

An individual can have one (or more than one) of nine responses to an experience. Jarvis describes nine routes on his learning cycle, which he puts into three groups: non learning, non reflective learning and reflective learning.

Non learning

Presumption (aspects 1-4)

This happens routinely in everyday life, where we experience the same (or similar) things many times as we socialise with those around us. We approach such situations in a similar way based on our previous experiences. In these situations we can assume we already know what to do or how to behave when, of course, this may not be the case.

Non-consideration (aspects 1-4)

Many learning opportunities are missed because we simply do not consider them to be noteworthy at the time: maybe we are too busy, too tired, distracted or simply see them as a waste of time.

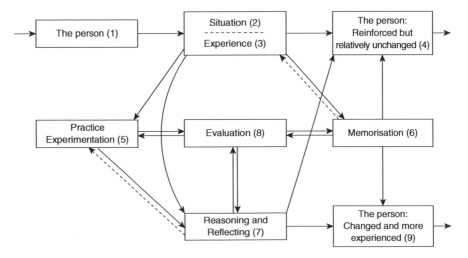

Figure 4.7 Jarvis' experiential learning cycle
Source: Jarvis (2006), p. 9

Rejection (aspects 1-3, then 7-9)

Here, something is specifically rejected; this involves some thought, followed by evaluation. There are a number of reasons why we reject things, for example we might feel they apply only to others and not to us. We might have tried them before and found them to be unhelpful. Over time it could be that rejection becomes part of our habitual response (we have all met cynical practitioners who are quick to say 'we've tried that before and it didn't work, so it won't work now') and hence rejection might over time become presumption.

Non-reflective learning

Pre-conscious (aspects 1-3 to either 4 or 9)

This learning happens incidentally and is generally not recognised as learning per se. In effect, it might not be called learning at all until it is recognised as such later. So we may not initially realise that we have learned something, but only see it like this later when it enters our consciousness. For example, we may recognise something as familiar (e.g. a theoretical model that seems very clear and simple, even obvious to us) which we later realise we have learned through a previous experience or experiences. It is a mistake to think of this as intuition ('well, I just knew how to do this' or 'I understood that anyway'); it has been learned previously because you can probably identify a time when you could not do the thing you have identified or did not understand it.

Practice (aspects 1-3, then 5-8 to 6 to either 4 or 9)

This often applies to skills learning. Through experience we have the opportunity to try things out in practice; this might include following processes and procedures, applying a theoretical model or copying an experienced practitioner as they model their skills to us. This is often done through conscious imitation of the practice of someone else whose work we respect and admire.

Memorisation (aspects 1-3 to 6, possibly to 8 and then to either 4 or 9)

Many of us will equate this to things that we have needed to learn 'off by heart', for example our times tables, mathematical formulae, chords on a guitar or keys on the computer keyboard. Here, repetition is important to ensure that our responses become automatic in relevant situations.

Reflective learning

Contemplation (route 1-3, to 7 to 8 to 6 to 9)

This could be described as purely thinking about something after an experience. Those with a strong Reflector learning style will be very familiar with this and can indeed spend a long time in contemplation. It does not necessarily mean that action will follow, although it might at some point in the future.

Reflective practice (route 1–3, possibly to 5, to 7 to 5 to 8 to 6 to 9)

This is clearly the most complex route so far as the practitioner reflects before experimentation and afterwards too and evaluates their experiences in an iterative way in order to become more skilful and knowledgeable. This underlines that reflective practice itself is indeed a complex process.

Experimental learning (route 1–3, to 7 to 5 to 7 to 8 to 6 to 9)

This appears more complex still as the learner focuses on practice as a basis for their reflections as they seek to ground their knowledge in practice and reality.

Perhaps the most important aspects here are the insights this work gives us about why we fail to learn. The following case study shows how an individual can navigate the cycle and fail to learn from experience.

Case study 4.4

Sarah is training to be a Careers Adviser who cannot understand why her learning appears to be 'stalling'. She doesn't understand why she keeps making the same mistakes. She knows what she needs to do and when she goes into the assessment, it's clear, but when it comes to it, she just doesn't seem able to do what she knows she needs to do. Following an in-depth discussion with her tutor it appears that she was 'tracking' across the cycle following each experience (3) because of failing to engage with any other element on the cycle. She was thereby exiting the cycle prematurely, reinforced (and determined to try again) but relatively unchanged (4). This is rather like the person in Figure 4.3.

Aspect 2 is particularly interesting and points to the influence that our situation has on our learning. It is clear that we learn more in some situations than in others, and, in this particular instance, the fact that Sarah was being assessed may well have an impact on how much (or rather how little) she could learn from the experience. We all need to be in environments that are conducive to learning to be able to develop to our full potential. In this particular case, she knows what she has to do, but somehow is unable to do it in the pressurised atmosphere of being assessed. So another possible response she might have could be to memorise what she has to do (6) to enable her to cope with the pressure. This might help a little, particularly if the assessment task is fairly straightforward, but even so, she could again exit the cycle reinforced but relatively unchanged (4) if she then fails to put things into practice.

Sarah could also spend some time in contemplation, thinking through the best ways of trying to achieve what she needed to achieve, but could still fail to change the way she does things and exit the cycle as before (4).

Table 4.1 Learning from experience

Likely to learn	Less likely to learn
We feel relatively comfortable	We feel uncomfortable
Relaxed but not too relaxed	Nervous, even fearful
Supported by others	Criticised by others
Focused	Unfocused or distracted
Open minded	'Blinkered'
Willing to try something new	Stuck in my usual ways of doing things
A positive environment	A negative environment
Positive personal circumstances	Negative personal circumstances

It is clear that we do not always learn from experience and there are many factors that can influence whether or not we learn at particular times in particular places. Table 4.1 highlights some of these.

Reflective activity 4.5

Now think about how you feel you learn best. Consider the points in the table above – which do you feel apply most to you and your learning? Are there any that do not apply? Are there any points you would like to add?

Reflective activity 4.6

Think of a time when you feel you learned a lot. Why was this? What can you gather from this about how you learn best?

Regressive transformation

As well as failing to learn from experience, Illeris (2014) identifies that people can fall back in their development through regressive transformation. Feelings of discomfort can be an indication that this is happening and thoughts such as the ones listed below can be common.

- That things are moving too quickly.
- That the demands are too high.
- That it is too difficult to let go of current viewpoints or behaviours.
- That the levels of doubt and uncertainty being demanded are too difficult to cope with.
- That we want to experience the safety and security of our current position and do not want to change.

Any or all of these feelings can mean that we fail to move forward in our learning and development.

Case study 4.5

Shan is a youth support worker who has completed her foundation degree. She now wants to move on to the final part of her studies to gain a full BA with honours. Shan is very committed to her work and study, but it seems that as soon as she returns to university things start to go wrong, and she feels like her development is regressing. In particular, her personal circumstances become difficult. Her parents emigrated last year; Shan's grandmother has become ill and she feels responsible for her as she is the relative who lives nearby. In addition, Shan's workload has recently increased because several members of staff have left her organisation and it is taking a while to recruit new people. Shan feels very tired and overwhelmed; since Christmas she has been ill on several occasions. This means that she has had to miss several sessions at university and feels she is falling behind. In spite of her supportive tutors, she decides to interrupt her studies as things at the current time are just too difficult for her. She hopes to resume her studies when things get easier for her at which point she hopes her development will be re-kindled.

Conclusion

In this chapter we have examined the whole area of learning from experience and have considered how and why this does not always happen. We have examined models by Kolb, Driscoll and Jarvis and have considered a range of factors that can promote or inhibit learning. In the next chapter we move on to consider some of the different arguments regarding how we learn most.

References

Borton, T. (1970) *Reach, Touch and Teach*, London: Hutchinson.
Driscoll, J. (ed.) (2007) *Practising Clinical Supervision: A Reflective Approach for Healthcare Professionals*, Edinburgh: Ballière Tindall, Elsevier.
Honey, P. and Mumford, A. (2000) *The Learning Styles Helper's Guide*, Maidenhead: Peter Honey Publications.
Illeris, K. (2014) *Transformative Learning and Identity*, Abingdon: Routledge.
Jarvis, P. (2003) 'Adult learning processes', in P. Jarvis and C. Griffin (eds) *Adult and Continuing Education*, London: Routledge, pp. 180–98.
Jasper, M. (2013) *Beginning Reflective Practice*, Andover: Cengage Learning.
Kolb, D. (1984) *Experiential Learning: Experience as the Source of Learning and Development*, Upper Saddle River, NJ: Prentice Hall.
Schön, D.A. (1983) *The Reflective Practitioner*, Aldershot: Ashgate.
Taylor, E.W. (2009) 'Fostering transformative learning', in J. Mezirow, E.W. Taylor et al. (eds) *Transformative Learning in Practice: Insights from Community, Workplace and Higher Education*, San Francisco, CA: Jossey-Bass.
Thompson, N. (2005) 'Reflective Practice', in R. Harrison and C. Wise (eds) *Working with Young People*, London: Sage.

5 Learning from positives and negatives
Critical incidents

'You've got to accentuate the positive, eliminate the negative.'

(Johnny Mercer, 1944)

Introduction

In the previous chapter our focus was on learning from experience, and how we do this has been the topic of much discussion and debate. For example, what kinds of experiences help us to maximise our learning? Many writers suggest that we learn most from things that we find difficult, for example things that 'go wrong' or do not go according to plan. Such approaches focus on issues connected with problem solving and are often referred to as 'deficit models'. Others advocate that we need to focus on the positives in order to learn from what is working well. In this chapter, two particular models are highlighted: one that focuses on problem solving and the other, advocating a more holistic approach, emphasising the positive. Events that are significant in our learning are often referred to as critical incidents and this is where this chapter begins as we now move on to consider how we can reflect at a deeper level about our practice.

What is a critical incident?

Many professionals in a wide range of settings use the technique of critical incident analysis in their practice in order to reflect at a deeper level about their work. Having considered how we can reflect on our work through learning from experience (see Chapter 4), we now need to delve deeper in order to begin to analyse and critically evaluate our practice, thereby moving from reflection towards critical reflection.

Initially used by Flanagan (1954) whilst diagnosing problems experienced by aircraft pilots, the term critical incident is often used in health settings where a patient's condition can become critical, sometimes very quickly. However, many professionals find the term useful when thinking about what they can learn from particular situations they face in their day-to-day practice. Such incidents may not always be critical in the literal sense of the word, although for professionals who work in very challenging situations they can be.

When seeking to identify what constitutes a critical incident, the following questions can give us some pointers.

- How do I feel? This will be examined in some depth in the next chapter, but our feelings often give us a good initial indication as to whether an incident is critical or not. We might feel irritated, angry, anxious or disturbed and have the kind of discomfort high-lighted by Driscoll (2007) when he asks if we feel troubled in any way in Step 2 of his cycle (see Chapter 4).

- Is this what I expected? Often an incident becomes critical when we are surprised by events and things do not turn out as we expect. This means that we need to examine our assumptions (see Chapter 7) to try and identify why we expected certain things to happen and not others.

- What do I do now? Critical incidents can 'stop us in our tracks' and make us question how we should proceed. This is particularly the case when we are new to practice and we can find ourselves thinking 'How do I handle this? or 'What on earth do I do now?' This is because such an incident highlights some kind of gap in our knowledge and experience.

- Other people seem to be able to cope with this, so why am I finding this so challenging? It is important to remember that an incident is only critical from the perspective of the particular individual. Something that you may find difficult, others may find easy and vice versa. This is because each of us has different levels of experience, but also we have all had different experiences in our past that can affect how we see things in the here and now. Such things can be discussed in the safety of supervision (see Chapter 8), assuming, of course, that this is available.

Several tools for critical incident analysis have been developed for use in different settings and they have the following areas in common regarding how an incident can be analysed effectively.

1   An account of the incident (often written) to start the process of analysis.
2   My initial responses and the responses of those around me.
3   The issues and dilemmas that this incident highlights.
4   The learning that I take from the incident.
5   Outcomes from the incident.

Reflective activity 5.1

Now think of a recent incident that you would describe as critical. Use the five head-ings above to help you to examine it.

Case study 5.1

Luke is training to be an occupational therapist and is enjoying his placement at a reha-bilitation centre for people who have suffered severe strokes. He gets on very well with a particular patient who jokingly discloses that he has been trying to walk on his own and, as a result, has had a few falls in his room. Luke knows that the patient should not

(continued)

(continued)

be doing this as he could injure himself. He feels anxious and uncomfortable when he discusses this with the patient, particularly when the patient then asks him not to tell anyone else. Luke promises that he will not say anything if the patient agrees not to try and walk again without help. Luke takes some time to write about this following his shift, and still feels very uncomfortable with the situation. He realises that he doesn't know enough about the situation and that he could be preventing better care. He feels that he does need to tell a manager and that he should not have promised to say nothing. He decides to go back to the patient concerned and explains to him that he needs to inform a manager. Luke explains to the patient that he has his health and recovery in mind and wants him to be able to go home as soon as possible, as he knows this is what the patient wants too. The patient accepts that Luke needs to disclose the details of the conversation and decides that he would prefer to disclose this himself with Luke's support, as this will also help him to communicate his frustrations regarding his progress.

The problematic experience

Writing from the perspective of education, Osterman and Kottkamp (2004) argue that we learn most from experiences that are problematic; hence, this is where our focus should be. They see reflective practice as a way of 'overcoming organizational habit and facilitating significant change' (Osterman and Kottkamp, 2004: 23).

As professional practitioners we can face a wide range of challenges in our practice, such as:

- Needing to meet targets possibly at the expense of meeting the needs of the people we are supporting.
- Pleasing our managers at the expense of our colleagues or clients.
- Keeping within budgets whilst also coping with high levels of demand for our time and work.
- Wanting to be seen as professionally competent whilst maintaining our integrity.
- Day to day situations that we find difficult to deal with.

Osterman and Kottkamp put forward an experiential learning cycle with many similarities to the work of Kolb (1984) (they based their work on his cycle), but also some key differences. The first step on the cycle is Problem Identification (as distinct from Concrete Experience); this emerges from practice when, for example, a particular outcome is not what was desired or expected. Just like a critical incident, this reveals a gap in our knowledge and practice. Such experiences present themselves as problems that demand our attention and make us want to work towards a possible solution by engaging in a learning process.

In these situations it can be tempting to skip to solutions (rather like the person in Figure 4.2, or the person who 'tracks' across the top of Jarvis', 2003 cycle, Figure 4.7) instead of taking the time to analyse what happened. Hence the second step on the cycle, Observation and Analysis, is seen to be the most important step and the most complex. Here, Osterman and Kottkamp delve into the realm of assumptions using Argyris' (1982)

Ladder of Inference (see Chapter 7). This asks us to analyse carefully what took place and to question our perspectives. They helpfully use the metaphor of lenses to show how the same thing can be seen in different ways depending on the lens we chose to look through, like for example when we use a camera. It is also important to remember that lenses can, of course, be clouded or distorted. This step on the cycle involves observing and analysing the situation and ourselves, thereby taking 'a dual stance being, on the one hand, the actor in a drama and, on the other hand, the critic who sits in the audience watching and analysing the whole performance' (Osterman and Kottkamp, 2004: 23).

Observation and Analysis is followed by Abstract Reconceptualization (as distinct from Abstract Conceptualization in Kolb's cycle) as we re-think our ways of thinking and acting. Here, new ideas and possible practices emerge through a deeper understanding of the situation and the event. As a result we reconceptualise; that is, we begin to think about the event differently, giving us new thoughts and ideas which can be transferred into different strategies for action that we can try out in the final step on the cycle, Active Experimentation.

Case study 5.2

Errol is training to be a Maths teacher in a secondary school and is finding some aspects of the work challenging. In particular, having always enjoyed Maths himself, he finds it difficult when some students do not seem to be interested in his lessons. The behaviour of the students can then become difficult to manage and before long Errol starts to dread particular lessons, particularly those on a Friday afternoon. Errol discusses this with his mentor who helps him to identify the problem. They then spend some time analysing the problem from a number of different angles. As a result, Errol begins to understand that his expectations of some of the students are too high and that many of the concepts he is trying to put across are abstract. He decides to use more concrete examples in his explanations and sets tasks that are much more practical and applied in his next lesson. In addition, he asks the students to discuss their work in pairs and to mark one another's work. Errol enjoys facilitating the lesson and, towards the end, tasks are discussed in a plenary session where he can assess what each student has learned. As he goes through the tasks with them, he asks the students to write on their own work so that he can be sure that they understand if they went wrong and how they could improve.

Critiques of Osterman and Kottkamp's work are similar to those of Kolb as, again, the cycle shows four steps, one following the other in a particular sequence. Of course, as we know, things do not always happen in such a neat and tidy fashion. In addition, the model is based on the assumption that a problem can be identified, but in practice that will not always be the case as sometimes we might struggle to see beyond the event itself, depending on our perspective and our previous experiences. It is important to emphasise that the model also seems to demand that we see ourselves as part of the problem. When analysing problems we need to be careful not only to see other things connected with the situation and other people as the problem, as this could mean that our observations and analysis are flawed. Like other reflective models, this model demands that we engage in critiquing ourselves as well as others and the situation itself.

Osterman and Kottkamp's model could be described as a deficit model. Such models can give the impression that we can only learn from problems or from things that go wrong. Without careful consideration, we can forget to look at aspects of our professional practice where things are going well.

Reflective activity 5.2

Now think about a problematic experience you have had recently and analyse it using Osterman and Kottkamp's cycle.

Learning from positive experiences

Written from the perspective of positive psychology and appreciative enquiry, Ghaye's (2011) work takes a different stance and argues that we need to focus on positive experiences as a source for learning and development. Only paying attention to problems or negative experiences can trap us in negative cycles of thinking, thereby making us too pessimistic about our work and trapped in what he calls 'deficit based actions' (Ghaye, 2011: 9). An emphasis on the positive can do much to motivate us and encourages us to capitalise on what is working well.

Ghaye (2011: 2) describes his reflective approach as 'strengths based' and, in contrast to Osterman and Kottkamp, he states clearly that 'It is not always necessary to first analyse the problematic aspects of the situation/experience'. He puts forward the following six key ideas in relation to reflection.

1   It is linked to practice and can help us to develop new ideas for high quality work.
2   It is linked with our feelings (see Chapter 6).
3   It is often structured and organized.
4   It often focuses on looking back on past experiences, but should also consider what is happening in the present.
5   It plays an important part in helping us to see what we are good at, what we can achieve and how we can improve.
6   It can be triggered by many different things, particularly questions we can pose in relation to our practice (see below).

Ghaye discusses four different kinds of reflection. The first two, reflection-in-action and reflection-on-action, are familiar (see Chapter 1). The other two types of reflection may not be familiar yet and they are as follows.

- Reflection-for-action – he describes this as fundamental. He argues that such reflection is undertaken for a particular reason, such as because we want to understand something better, or to develop something or improve it. It is done as part of a process of planning how to address a particular issue.
- Reflection-with-action. The focus here is on thinking that leads to action. This looks forward to things you might do as an individual or with other people in a team.

Ghaye argues that as well as looking back on situations and experiences (reflection-on-action), we also need to examine the present (reflection-in-action) and look to the future (reflection-for action and reflection-with-action).

Ghaye's strengths-based model offers an approach that encourages us to build on the positives by asking the following questions.

- What is successful right now? (Appreciate)
- What do we need to change to make things better? (Imagine)
- How can we achieve this? (Design)
- Who needs to take action and what will the consequences be? (Act).

In contrast to other cycles, the points above are presented at various places on the capital letter R as shown in Figure 5.1.

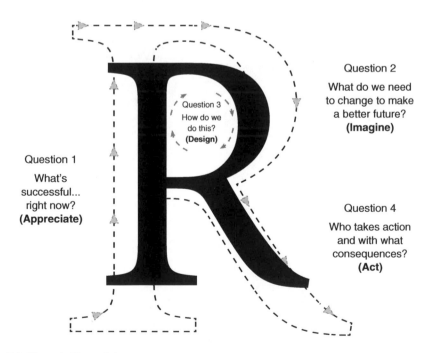

Figure 5.1 Ghaye's R model
Source: Ghaye (2011), p. 18

Case study 5.3

Catherine is training to be a counsellor and is finding certain aspects of this challenging, in particular the role-playing activities. She is always quick to see where she feels she has gone wrong, and in discussion finds it very difficult to say what she is doing well. She discusses this with her supervisor who suggests that she uses Ghaye's model to help her to identify what she does well. Catherine writes the following reflections in her journal.

- What is successful right now? I am finding the role plays easier now. Today I asked lots of open questions and felt much more relaxed. I know I can communicate well and that people enjoy talking to me. It's easier when you know people and the students in my group are all very supportive.
- What do we need to change to make things better? Practice, practice, practice. I know this is how I will get better.
- How can we achieve this? I need to find more opportunities to practice using my skills because I'm sure this will help my confidence.
- Who needs to take action and what will the consequences be? Tomorrow I'll go to the volunteering fair and find out if I can do some voluntary work as I think meeting new people will help. I might be able to get some relevant experience too. I've also got to know two people well on my course and one of them has suggested we could get together to practice our skills. This is a good idea and I'll ask if we can arrange this.

Ghaye's work provides a useful antidote to many models of reflection that emphasise that we should focus on problems. It seems fair to say that if we only focus on problems or things that go wrong, we can forget the things we do well. This can trap us in negative ways of thinking about our practice, which can be very de-motivating in the longer term. We all need to remember times when we recognise things we have done well as this builds our career happiness (Bassot, Barnes and Chant, 2014) and is important for how we feel about ourselves and our work. The R model itself is clear and easy to remember because it stands out as being different from other cyclical models that are presented as being circular or oval in shape.

However, it is important to remember that focusing too much on the positive can make us too accepting of our practice and can lead us to overestimate how effective our practice actually is – in effect another distortion of the metaphorical mirror (see Chapter 2). This can make us unaware of the things we could have done better. In spite of the focus on positives, Ghaye still speaks of improving practice and making it better, when perhaps to use the term *even better* would be more appropriate.

Reflective activity 5.3

Now think about a positive experience you have had recently and analyse it using Ghaye's cycle.

Reflective activity 5.4

Now look back at your notes on Activity 5.2 and compare what you wrote. Which model have you found the most useful and why?

Conclusion

In this chapter we have discussed two contrasting models of reflection – one focusing on problems and the other on positive experiences. It seems clear that there is a place for both in the daily challenges of professional practice. Focusing only on problems can 'weigh us down' and make us think that our practice is never good enough. Focusing only on positives can deceive us into thinking that what we did was good in the circumstances when it could be significantly improved. A careful balance seems appropriate, and selecting a model for reflection for particular circumstances is just one part of the professional judgement of practitioners. In the next chapter we move on to consider the whole area of engaging with our feelings.

References

Argyris, C. (1982) *Reasoning, Learning and Action: Individual and Organizational*, San Francisco: Jossey-Bass.

Bassot, B., Barnes, A. and Chant, A. (2014) *A Practical Guide to Career Learning and Development: Innovation in Careers Education 11–19*, Abingdon: Routledge.

Driscoll, J. (ed.) (2007) *Practising Clinical Supervision: A Reflective Approach for Healthcare Professionals*, Edinburgh: Ballière Tindall, Elsevier.

Flanagan, J.C. (1954) 'The critical incident technique', *Psychology Bulletin*, 51: 327–58.

Ghaye, T. (2011) *Teaching and Learning through Reflective Practice: A Practical Guide for Positive Action*, Abingdon: Routledge.

Jarvis, P. (2003) 'Adult learning processes', in P. Jarvis and C. Griffin (eds) *Adult and Continuing Education*, London: Routledge, pp. 180–98.

Kolb, D. (1984) *Experiential Learning: Experience as the Source of Learning and Development*, NJ: Prentice Hall.

Mercer, J. (1944) *Accentuate the Positive*. Available from http://www.lyricsmania.com/accentuate_the_positive_lyrics_johnny_mercer.html. Accessed 7 May 2015.

Osterman, K.F. and Kottkamp, R.B. (2004) *Reflective Practice for Educators*, 2nd edn., Thousand Oaks, CA: Corwin Press.

6 Engaging with emotions

'If you are carrying strong feelings about something that happened in your past, they may hinder your ability to live in the present.'

(Les Brown, 1992)

Introduction

Many writers on the subject of critical reflection discuss the importance of engaging with our feelings. This is particularly the case when reading literature from health and social care, where some of the challenges practitioners face can prompt an emotional response. This chapter will explore the topics of objectivity and subjectivity, and the importance of engaging with our emotions will be discussed. The reasons for doing this will be explored using insights from Transactional Analysis. This is followed by an explanation of the Almond Effect. Two theoretical models will then be presented that can help us to engage with our feelings in a systematic way. The chapter concludes with some suggestions of how we can begin to process our feelings effectively.

What are emotions?

First, it is important to understand what emotions are and the effects they can have on us. Emotions are more than just feelings; Williams and Penman (2011: 19) define them as a combination of thoughts, feelings, impulses and bodily sensations (such as a faster heart rate or trembling hands) that create 'an overall guiding theme or state of mind'. These different elements play off one against the other and can result in us feeling positive or negative depending on the situation and our previous experiences. Our emotions, therefore, guide us in particular directions depending on the circumstances we are facing. Unlike many animals, who are able to experience such things as fear (for example, when chased by a predator) and then quickly relax, as humans we tend to dwell on what happened as our minds remember past experiences that are similar and imagine what might happen in similar circumstances in the future. The result is that we remain on high alert and can find it difficult to 'switch off' when we leave work.

Objectivity and subjectivity

When looking at definitions of these terms in a standard dictionary, objectivity is said to rely on facts and subjectivity on opinion. Objectivity is often linked with the idea of taking a scientific approach that can be justified and defended if needed, whereas subjectivity is more difficult to define and relies on deciding how to act in the particular situation depending on the circumstances. Many professional practitioners seek to take an objective approach to their work by being clear about factual events and circumstances, trying not to rely on opinion, which can be biased either in favour of or against the client. However, Schön (1983) suggests that people in the 'minor professions' need to move away from a reliance on a scientific approach (or technical rationality) to reflection-in-action (see Chapter 1). This kind of 'thinking on your feet' can often involve engaging with our emotions in our everyday practice.

Why is it important to consider our emotions in relation to professional practice?

Many people enter the so-called 'helping professions' because they enjoy relating to people and feel that they have something to give both on a personal and societal level. Any such work is demanding as it involves getting closer to people's lived experiences and seeking to support them. In addition, many clients face struggles and setbacks that we can only imagine, although some practitioners may indeed have had similar experiences and feel drawn into their particular role because of them. For example, my own lack of careers advice coupled with my choice of the 'wrong' course at university certainly prompted me into my work as a Careers Adviser; my doctoral research was all about university choice and even today it gives me great satisfaction to help someone choose the 'right' course or career for them.

However, because of these experiences, working with clients can bring our past experiences, positive and negative, into focus. A counsellor friend of mine once explained it like this. If you imagine the human brain as an oval-shaped object, the top third of the oval represents our conscious – the things (including thoughts, memories and experiences) that we remember and are aware of on a regular basis. The bottom two thirds are our unconscious – a myriad of things that we are not aware of. What appears at first to be a complete barrier between the two (see Figure 6.1) in fact has a concealed trap door in the middle (see Figure 6.2) which opens in response to triggers that are beyond our control. These triggers are things that remind us of our past experiences and can include such things as sights, sounds, smells, words and phrases. When we experience a trigger, the trap door opens and things from our unconscious 'spill out' into our conscious; Freud (1912) called this 'transference'.

But how is this connected with our emotions? In his work on Transactional Analysis (TA), Berne (1961) asserts that the human brain stores memories and feelings in such a way that they are inseparable. This means that we not only remember things that have happened in the past, but we also experience the feelings again that we felt at the time. In short, we not only remember the past event, we also feel how we felt at that time.

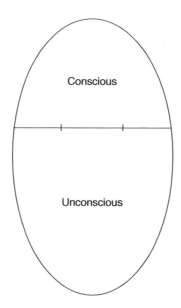

Figure 6.1 The human brain

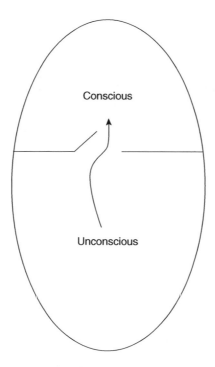

Figure 6.2 The human brain responding to a 'trigger'

Berne argues that everything we experience is stored within us. When hearing this for the first time, this might seem somewhat far-fetched, but here are two examples that serve to illustrate Berne's point.

A colleague of mine who used to teach in a university in Sweden once came to visit my university and as part of his visit observed one of my sessions. That day I was teaching Berne's TA and as we discussed some of the core principles, he shared this story. He explained that he grew up in the locality of my university and as he travelled that morning by taxi he was suddenly overcome by an intense feeling of travel sickness. By the time he reached the university the feeling had passed; as he had not experienced any kind of travel sickness for a long time, he was curious about this. By the time of the session, he had remembered being a very small boy (about 3 years old) and being in the car with a relative and feeling very travel sick, so much so that they had to stop the car – and you can imagine the rest! That morning, his feelings of being travel sick occurred at the very spot where they had had to stop the car that day many years before.

Again whilst teaching TA, I once asked my students if any of them wanted to share an experience to illustrate the premise that memories and feelings are stored together. One student explained that she was a foster carer and one of the teenage girls that she used to care for had a real dislike of oranges. This dislike was so intense they could not have any oranges, orange juice or anything containing oranges in the house. One day the student concerned spoke to the girl's social worker about this and it transpired that in her case notes it was recorded that she had been abandoned as a newborn baby and left outside a hospital in an orange box.

When thinking about the effect of triggers, it is important to remember that memories cannot be recalled without the feelings experienced and vice versa. Harris (1967: 12) explained it in this way 'I not only remember how I felt, I feel the same way now'. This means that as professional practitioners we should not be surprised when we have emotional responses to our experiences at work. Often these will occur as a result of a trigger reminding us of a past experience (positive or negative) which in turn will mean that we also feel how we felt at that time.

Reflective activity 6.1

Describe a recent experience that prompted an emotional response. What surprised you about this?

Case study 6.1

Tom is a bereavement counsellor who is working with a number of clients who have recently lost people close to them. He enjoys his work and went into it because of his own experiences of losing his father when he was young. At that time Tom was fortunate in having a close relationship with his father's district nurse, who was also the

(continued)

(continued)

father of one of his close school friends. Tom spent time talking very informally with him for a period of time following his father's death and some years later realised how valuable this had been in supporting him and helping him begin to come to terms with a wide range of things that he had thought and felt during this time. Tom is currently working with a client in her fifties who has recently lost her elderly mother. During their early sessions Tom is surprised by his feelings about the client and her situation. The client's mother was 85 when she died and Tom felt jealous and wished that his father had lived such a long life. He felt that the client should have been grateful for her mother's long life, but instead she was overwhelmed by grief. He found himself thinking 'if you knew what I went through, you'd realise how lucky you are and get through it'. Tom's grief that he felt many years ago re-surfaced, and in that moment he felt like he did during those first few months after his father died.

So if the trapdoor is open, what happens next?

The Almond Effect and the closing of the trapdoor

As human beings most of us have emotional responses to the situations we encounter and the people around us, which can be triggered by a range of things. The effect this has can sometimes be very powerful and can take us by surprise. We can all probably remember times when we have said things that we very quickly regret, or have reacted in a certain way and wish we had done things differently. In her book *Where Did That Come From?* Riches (2012) explains that this happens because of what she calls The Almond Effect.

Neuroscience shows that the human brain responds to potentially threatening situations with a 'flight or fight' response. These responses are mostly automatic and result from the hardwiring of our neural pathways. Developed through the process of evolution, they have played an important part in the survival of the human race. Originating from the Greek word for almond, the amygdalae are two almond-shaped parts of the brain that play a vital role in both stimulating and regulating our emotional reactions to people and situations, particularly in relation to fear. The amygdalae prompt our 'fight or flight' response where appropriate; they also enable us to sense emotional responses in other people. It is important to remember that our instinctive emotional responses always happen first; this is the Almond Effect.

However, the process does not usually stop there. Following our initial emotional response, we can then reach a more rational approach by using a range of strategies, many of which involve helping us to slow down and think. First, of course, we have to recognise what is happening as it is happening (part of the skill of reflection-in-action, Schön, 1983). These signs will vary from person to person but could mean being aware of such things as an increase in our heart rate, trembling, nausea or shallow breathing. This recognition gives us the opportunity to slow down and to reach a more measured response. Riches suggests some practical techniques such as remembering to breathe deeply and being sure to keep our body language open so as not to appear defensive. Following this process the trapdoor closes.

Reflective activity 6.2

Think back to the previous activity. Following your initial response, did you manage to reach a more rational one? If so how? If not, why not?

Case study 6.2

Bernadette is training to be a Careers Adviser and as part of her course she is required to spend some time on placement in a school. She decided to become a Careers Adviser because she had very little guidance when she was at school. She left school at 16 because she hated it and drifted from job to job until she found something she enjoyed. She now has two children of her own and wants them, and young people generally, to get more support than she did. Bernadette is not looking forward to her school placement and after the first week she contacts her tutor as she is very unhappy. She explains that each time she goes into school she feels physically sick and cannot wait for the end of the day. In particular, she cannot bear the smell of the school, which 'hits' her as soon as she walks through the main entrance. She feels that she might have to withdraw from the course, or work with adult clients instead, as she cannot bear the thought of feeling like this in the long term. During the discussion Bernadette is reminded of her sessions on TA and realises that her unhappy memories of school are re-surfacing, in particular how she was always in trouble and made to stand outside the Head's office. The smell is acting as a trigger for her memories and feelings, making her fearful and wanting to 'flee'. Bernadette soon realises that she is an adult and does not need to experience her time in school now in this way. She also realises that she has lots of empathy with young people in school who might be having similar experiences to hers, and that she is in a good position to support them.

Of course, all of this is also very helpful when thinking about how our clients respond; being in tune with our own emotions and recognising and understanding the emotions of others are two key aspects of emotional intelligence (Goleman, 1996). In relation to work with clients, it is important to remember two things. First, that the initial response we see is likely to be an emotional one. The second is that some clients will need our help and support to reach a more rational response and will not always be able to do this for themselves. At times, we too will need this kind of support from colleagues, and through supervision if it is available.

Reflective activity 6.3

How might you be able to use your knowledge of the Almond Effect when working with your clients?

Why do we need to process our feelings?

Processing our feelings can be uncomfortable and, particularly when we are busy, it can be very tempting to simply put them to one side. However, being in tune with our emotions is an important part of professional practice because it allows us to deal with how we are feeling about our work and those we are supporting. Many practitioners experience positive and negative emotions about their work, and the effect of not processing our feelings, particularly negative ones, can be damaging and detrimental to ourselves and to the people we are supporting.

For example, a practitioner who has lots of negative feelings about their work and their clients can expect to experience at least some of the following.

- Lack of motivation.
- Dissatisfaction with work.
- Higher levels of anxiety.
- Fatigue – especially mental and emotional fatigue – which in extreme cases can lead to exhaustion.
- Cynicism.
- Anger.
- Anxiety.
- Burn out.
- Low self esteem.
- Little sense of well being.
- In extreme cases burn out, depression and poor mental health.

Storing our feelings can be rather like using a 'pressure cooker'. As time goes on, unless the steam is released, the pan could explode, with somewhat devastating consequences.

Gibbs' reflective cycle

We will now move on to examine two theoretical models that can help us to process our feelings. The first is Gibbs' (1988) reflective cycle and is shown in Figure 6.3.

There are some clear similarities with Kolb's (1984) model (see Chapter 4) but also some clear differences. Like Kolb, Gibbs also emphasises learning that happens from experience, which he suggests happens in a particular sequence. Gibbs' cycle appears more detailed, having six steps and provides useful questions as prompts to help us to explore what we have learned at a deeper level. This also makes the model easy to use in practice.

At the second point on the cycle Gibbs focuses on feelings and our emotional response to situations. For those professionals supporting people in challenging circumstances (e.g. health, counselling, social work), this aspect of Gibbs' cycle is particularly helpful. Bearing in mind the Almond Effect and the ways in which our brains store memories, it would be somewhat naïve to think that as professional practitioners we could somehow turn our emotions off and respond objectively immediately.

Figure 6.3 Gibbs' reflective cycle

The third step on Gibbs' cycle is also worth noting. The questions under the heading of 'Evaluation' ask us to examine what was good about a particular experience as well as what was bad. This combination reminds us of the contrasting cycles of Ghaye (2011) and Osterman and Kottkamp (2004) (see Chapter 5) and seems well balanced. It prevents us from dwelling too much on the negative side and running ourselves down and also asks us to look at the positives so that we can build on them.

In particular, the fourth step on the cycle entitled 'Analysis' helps us to think at a deeper level still in order to try to make sense of the experience. This could involve looking at the experience from different perspectives to try to see what was happening and why. It is interesting to note that Gibbs chooses tentative words in his question for this step on the cycle 'What sense can you make of the situation?' rather than a more direct question like 'What sense do you make of the situation?' The implication here is that we will not always be able to make sense of every experience in our professional practice but he certainly encourages us to try.

In some situations it will be easy to stop at this particular point on the cycle, but the next two points are important if we are to learn from experience and if our practice is to move forward. Using the heading 'Conclusion' Gibbs encourages us to think through alternative approaches and what we might have been able to do differently. The cycle concludes with 'Action Plan' where he asks us to think about what we would do if the same situation arose again.

Case study 6.3

Prem is training to be a paediatric nurse and is enjoying his placement in an Accident and Emergency unit. One Saturday afternoon a couple arrive with their two-year-old son who is having difficulty breathing. They have been preparing for his birthday party and think he might have swallowed something, perhaps one of the party balloons. Prem assists the nurse involved but finds the situation quite distressing. He decides to use Gibbs' cycle to reflect on the experience after his shift.

Description – what happened? The parents arrived with their son who was having difficulty breathing. They were understandably very anxious and distressed. The boy looked a bit blue and was starting to become floppy.

Feelings – what were you thinking and feeling? I felt very anxious for the boy and for the parents too. I knew we needed to act quickly, but didn't know what to do. This made me panic inside, although I tried not to show it. I also felt angry because the boy's parents had not been watching him closely enough.

Evaluation – what was good and bad about the experience? I was glad that I was with an experienced nurse who knew what to do. She took action quickly and the boy was assessed by the registrar on duty and everything then moved very quickly to get him the help he needed. I found my own initial feelings of panic difficult to cope with and hope that I didn't pass them on to the boy and his parents.

Analysis – what sense can I make of the situation? I felt guilty because of my anger towards the parents. It is not possible to watch a two-year-old every minute - this could happen to anyone. I didn't have enough clinical skills or experience to cope with this. Maybe my anger was caused by a lack of understanding.

Conclusion – what else could I have done? I was pleased that I was able to manage my feelings of panic and did not appear to pass these on to the parents.

Action plan – if it arose again, what would I do? I would take some deep breaths, act swiftly and calmly to get the necessary help, try to understand the clients' situation and use my interpersonal skills to help them in the best way I can.

Reflective activity 6.4

Now choose a recent experience from your professional practice and reflect on it using the questions from Gibbs' cycle. How does using this cycle compare with others you have now used?

The work of Boud, Keogh and Walker

Boud, Keogh and Walker (1985) also encourage us to pay attention to our feelings, often referred to in literature as the affective dimension. Writing from the context of adult education, the focus once more is on learning from experience and they argue that reflection acts as a processing phase after the occurrence of an experience. Importantly, they also argue that it is the conscious process of reflection that enables us to learn and to develop our practice through analysis and evaluation rather than some kind of ad hoc thinking about things, for example on the bus on the way home. Such reflection can be prompted by positive and negative experiences and involves intellectual and affective aspects. The outcomes of reflection can include the following.

* Synthesis – a mixing of different ideas to bring about a different whole.
* Integration – combining two or more things to become more effective.
* Appropriation – taking something forward that you want to use in the future.
* Validation – growing confidence in knowing your actions were justifiable.
* A new affective state – a change in the way you feel about the experience.
* A decision to engage in some further activity and a commitment to action.

Boud et al. draw our attention to three important factors that affect learning, and it is worth considering them in relation to our own learning. First, learners all have previous experiences that affect how they approach the current learning situation. So, if someone has had positive learning experiences in the past, they may well be more enthusiastic and open to learning compared to those whose experiences of learning have been more negative. Those who have had negative experiences need an opportunity to process them; this is not only important for adults in an educational setting but for children too. Such negative experiences prompt emotional reactions, which, if not processed, can become a barrier to learning. Processing those feelings can mean liberation from previous assumptions, such as 'I'm no good at Maths'. Rather like Honey and Mumford's (2000) learning styles (see Chapter 2), we need to be aware of our learning habits so that, if necessary, we can liberate ourselves from them. This is a process that can be swift (like a 'eureka' moment) or slower, where a series of happenings enable us to look at things differently. For those in the teaching profession these are vital points to remember not only in relation to how we learn in our own practice, but also how those in our classrooms and seminars learn too.

Reflective activity 6.5

Take a few minutes to think about your previous experiences of education and learning. How might your learning habits affect your learning now?

Secondly, Boud et al. discuss the importance of the intent of the learner. People differ in how they approach learning; some are satisfied with a 'surface approach' (Boud et al., 1985: 24) whilst others adopt a deeper one. Those who take a deeper approach seek to understand what they are studying and engage with it, for example to compare and contrast it to what they know already. They actively interact with their material to discover meaning. Those who take a surface approach are more likely to memorise information and simply focus on the requirements of the essay or examination.

Thirdly, Boud et al. are clear that taking a reflective approach is a deliberate choice, rather like the choice we make to look in the 'metaphorical mirror' (see Chapter 1). Choosing to look in the 'metaphorical mirror' then presents us with a second choice: whether to take action on what we see or not. And, importantly, we must always be prepared for our initial emotional responses to what we see and be ready to process them.

Boud et al. present their model in three stages and these are shown in Figure 6.4.

Stage 1 (returning to the experience) is familiar and involves taking some time to reflect on the experience. Boud et al. suggest that writing things down in a detailed way can be helpful and they also encourage us to hold back from making any judgements regarding what happened at this point. In particular, they ask us to observe our feelings. This material provides us with the data that we need to process in the next stage.

Stage 2 (attending to feelings) asks us to pay attention to our feelings. Using positive feelings is important as these keep us focused on moving forward, particularly in circumstances that might be challenging. In very challenging situations our positive feelings might be minor compared to the negative feelings we experience and, therefore, all the more important to remember in relation to our own motivation and well being. This stage also involves processing our negative feelings to ensure that they do not 'drag us down' and become a barrier to our development.

Stage 3 (re-evaluating the experience) is closely linked with the outcomes of reflection on page 74, which lead us to action. This re-evaluation can help us to see things differently, to change our behaviour and to be ready to take action on what we have found.

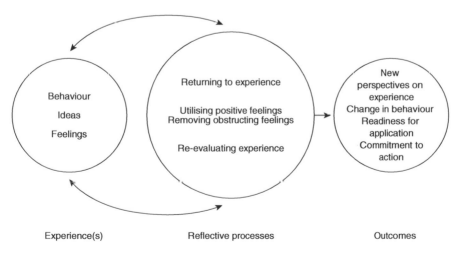

Figure 6.4 Boud et al.'s model for reflection

Source: Boud et al. (1985), p. 36

In particular, it is important to notice that, unlike previous reflective cycles we have examined, Boud et al. show that their cycle is multi-directional. In other words, the arrows go in more than one direction, showing that the processes involve re-visiting (perhaps even repeatedly) the stages, as distinct from other models that seem to imply that the stages or steps in a cycle are only visited once. This makes this cycle different and more complex.

Case study 6.4

Jon is on his second placement in a primary school and is working in a class with pupils in Year 1. He is getting to know the children quite well and can see that there are a couple of children in the class who might be being bullied by other children. Jon notices that there are certain boys and girls who call some of the other children by what he considers to be harmful nicknames and this makes him feel very uncomfortable. He uses Boud et al.'s cycle to analyse his experiences so he can discuss them in depth with his mentor. He writes this in his journal.

Stage 1 (returning to the experience) - Children can be very mean. Today I over-heard one of the girls teasing another girl because she is friends with one of the boys. She and the boy have been friends since nursery and she became very upset when the other girl started to call him silly rhyming names. I felt angry because good friendships are so important for children and bullying is never acceptable.

Stage 2 (attending to feelings) - Why did I feel so angry? I suppose it reminded me of the name I was often called at school and how it really hurt and often undermined my confidence. I wasn't bullied badly at school, but even so, calling people names is horrible. I remember talking to my Mum about it and that always made me feel better. She used to say 'sticks and stones may break my bones, but words will never hurt me'. I remembered those words and they helped me to feel better.

Stage 3 (re-evaluating the experience) - what new perspectives do I now have and how will I change my behaviour? Children can be cruel but I don't need to let that drag me down to the point where I feel negative about them. Bullying is never good, but children need to build their resilience and as long as they have support, they can often cope with it better. I will talk to my mentor and ask her to help me to formulate some strategies that I can use in situations like this.

How can we process our feelings effectively?

It is clear that processing our feelings is important and that it will be vital to our well being to find effective ways of doing this. Some possible ways include:

- Writing about your experiences in a notebook or journal. As discussed in Chapter 3, this forces us to slow down.
- Using a recording device (e.g. on your smart phone or tablet) that you can listen to afterwards.
- Finding a trusted colleague who you can share with; often this is termed a critical friend (see Chapter 8).
- Using supervision if it is available (see Chapter 8).
- Finding a safe space, e.g. a supportive group, where you can share your feelings and know that they will be handled sensitively.

All of these things will help you to externalise your feelings rather than store them up when they might have a tendency to make you re-visit things far too often. It is also important to remember that the feelings we have can be communicated unwittingly to other people; this is called countertransference.

Reflective activity 6.6

Which of these methods would suit you best? If appropriate, how can you make sure you have the support mechanism in place?

Case study 6.5

Camille is a newly qualified social worker who understands the value of reflection. She is working in a children and families team and has some challenging safeguarding issues to deal with, which she finds upsetting and sometimes distressing. Camille often finds it difficult to 'switch off' when she leaves work, so decides to use some methods to help her to process the feelings she is experiencing. She writes in her reflective journal regularly and finds that this is a good way of 'letting off steam'. When time is at a premium, she records her thoughts by speaking into her smart phone. She has a close friend at work and they have a regular cup of coffee together each week to share their experiences. Camille always attends her supervision sessions and uses these as a means of exploring her cases from a number of different angles. All of these help her to process her feelings and to externalise them. This means she is less likely to take them home with her and pass them on to other people.

Conclusion

In this chapter we have explored the vital area of engaging with our emotions in professional practice. This is always challenging, particularly in relation to processing negative feelings we all undoubtedly have at certain times. Finding ways of doing this that work for us as individuals is vital for our well being, motivation and development. In the next chapter we move on to consider the area of assumptions.

References

Berne, E. (1961) *Transactional Analysis in Psychotherapy*, New York: Grove Press.

Brown, L. (1992) *Live Your Dreams*, New York: HarperCollins Publishers, p. 16.

Boud, D., Keogh, R. and Walker, D. (1985) *Reflection: Turning Experience into Learning*, London: Routledge Falmer.

Freud, S. (1912) 'The dynamics of transference', in J. Strachey (ed.) (1961) *Standard Edition of the Complete Works of Sigmund Freud*, Vol. 12, London: Hogarth, pp. 99–108.

Gibbs, G. (1998) *Learning by Doing: A Guide to Teaching and Learning Methods*, Oxford: Further Education Unit, Oxford Polytechnic.

Ghaye, T. (2011) *Teaching and Learning through Reflective Practice: A Practical Guide for Positive Action*, Abingdon: Routledge.

Goleman, D. (1996) *Emotional Intelligence: Why It Can Matter More Than IQ*, London: Bloomsbury.

Harris, T.A. (1967) *I'm OK – You're OK*, New York: HarperCollins.

Honey, P. and Mumford, A. (2000) *The Learning Styles Helper's Guide*, Maidenhead: Peter Honey Publications.

Kolb, D. (1984) *Experiential Learning: Experience as the Source of Learning and Development*, New Jersey: Prentice Hall.

Osterman, K.F. and Kottkamp, R.B. (2004) *Reflective Practice for Educators*, 2nd edn., Thousand Oaks, CA: Corwin Press.

Riches, A. (2012) *"Where Did That Come From?" How to Keep Control in Any Situation* [e-book] Sudbury, MA: eBookIt. Available at http://www.anneriches.com.au/almond-effect.html.

Schön, D.A. (1983) *The Reflective Practitioner*, Aldershot: Ashgate.

Williams, M. and Penman, D. (2011) *Mindfulness: A Practical Guide to finding Peace in a Frantic World*, London: Piatkus.

7   Bringing assumptions to the surface

'We don't see things as they are, we see things as we are.'

(Cicero)

Introduction

In this chapter we will explore the area of assumptions including how they come about and why as professionals we need to understand some of the assumptions we might be making. We will examine different levels of assumptions and discuss some theoretical perspectives that can help us to understand more about how we can challenge our ways of thinking. The chapter will conclude with a model that can be used individually and in supervision to help us to reflect on how we can begin to overcome some of our limiting assumptions.

What are assumptions and how do they come about?

If we look up the word assumption in a basic dictionary we would find it defined as something that is accepted as true or certain to happen but is without proof. Assumptions are ideas and thoughts that evolve over time and become things that we then take for granted. They become so ingrained in our daily thoughts and actions that we no longer question their validity or even think about them. In some circumstances assumptions are valuable as they prevent us from needing to think about every aspect of our lives in detail. Sometimes these kinds of assumptions are referred to as working hypotheses. For example, if we had to think closely about what to do each time we did something as routine as making a cup of tea, life would be exhausting! Instead, we draw on our past experiences and make it somewhat automatically. However, other assumptions are not helpful, as they can lead to unconscious bias in our practice (Moss-Racusin, Dovidio, Brescoll, Graham and Handelsman, 2012).

Often, our assumptions are based on our personal values. Values are things that are important to us - in a literal sense they are things that we value. Our personal values are deep rooted and will often stem from our upbringing and can include things like, honesty, hard work and the importance of family. Personal values, therefore, reflect the social context of the individual and vary from person to person.

Reflective activity 7.1

Think about some of the phrases that you heard regularly when you were growing up. What do they say about your values?

Brookfield (1995: 2) describes critical reflection as a process of 'hunting assumptions'. Here, the word 'hunting' is particularly helpful and gives us insights into how difficult a process discovering some of our assumptions can be. Hunting usually involves searching out things that are hidden beneath the surface, and sometimes the things we are hunting positively want to escape from us. Brookfield (1995: 2) describes assumptions as 'taken-for-granted beliefs about the world and our place within it that seem so obvious as not to need stating explicitly'. He describes the following three levels of assumptions.

1   'Paradigmatic assumptions' – these operate at the deepest level and have become so ingrained that often we simply do not think about them. They play a vital part in how we structure what we see around us and in the way we view and experience the world. Our paradigmatic assumptions inform our views of 'reality' and 'truth' and are so deep that we do not necessarily even recognise them as assumptions. Many people resist examining them because the process can be very challenging and at times uncomfortable. Our paradigmatic assumptions inform the two other levels shown below and lead us to think and act in certain ways.

2   'Prescriptive assumptions' – these are based on what we think ought to happen in particular situations. For example, we may be working hard with a particular client and may feel that they should then take action on the things we have discussed. However, there may be many reasons why they do not take any action; we are simply assuming that they should do so.

3   'Causal assumptions' – these inform what we expect to happen or to be the case in certain situations. For example, I tried this particular approach in this situation and the outcome was good, so I am then surprised when it does not work in a similar situation. I might assume that the reason it failed is because of a lack of engagement on the part of others. Of course, this will not necessarily be the case.

Reflective activity 7.2

Now spend some time thinking about the kinds of assumptions you make in relation to your professional learning and practice. How would you categorise these using Brookfield's 3 levels?

Case study 7.1

Jude is a learning mentor in a secondary school and he supports students with challenging behaviour. He is currently working with a student (Melanie) who finds attending school very difficult and has frequent panic attacks. Despite lots of hard work, Jude

(continued)

(continued)

feels that she is not making much progress. He begins to wonder if he might be expecting too much of her and decides to examine his thoughts using Brookfield's levels of assumptions. He wrote this in his journal.

Causal assumptions – I really don't understand it. I've been working with Melanie for quite a while now, but she is still having lots of panic attacks. It's so distressing to watch and I really wonder how she will cope with everyday life. I've tried lots of different strategies to try and help her to calm down, but nothing really seems to work. When she gets anxious, the panic just seems to take over. I think she's just not trying hard enough.

Prescriptive assumptions – working with Melanie is getting more and more difficult. She says she is trying the strategies we have discussed, but says they're not working. She really should be getting better by now, but she's just getting worse.

Paradigmatic assumptions – I want Melanie to get better because then her life will be so much easier, and I guess mine will be too. I suppose I'm finding the fact that she isn't improving difficult because it makes me feel like I'm a failure. I'm not used to this. I'm used to being successful; people often praise me for my work, especially parents, and maybe deep down it feels like I am letting everyone down in some way. This puts pressure on me and maybe this means I put pressure on her. Perhaps I'm the one that needs to relax and listen more.

Why professionals need to understand the assumptions they may be making

Unless we give due attention to our assumptions, our professional practice could be likened to some kind of 'autopilot'. Of course, we cannot examine every detail of our working day – there is insufficient time and our working lives would then be too tiring mentally and emotionally. However, any kind of 'autopilot' is very risky for the following reasons.

- If we fail to consider the assumptions we are making about our clients (including such things as our prejudices and stereotypes), we can find ourselves practising in a discriminatory or oppressive way.
- If we always see what we believe we see, we do things in similar ways and our practice becomes stale. We fail to see positives when our assumptions are disconfirmed and our practice stagnates.
- If we practice 'in the same way' we lose our creativity.
- We risk going back to the area of 'unconscious incompetence' (see Chapter 1).

How assumptions can be questioned

In many circumstances our feelings act as a guide to the assumptions we might be making and these will often be closely linked with our previous experiences. Table 7.1 shows some examples of a range of different feelings we might have in relation to particular

Table 7.1 Feelings we might have in relation to particular circumstances in our professional practice

Feeling	Past experience	Assumption about the future
Discouraged	Working hard with a particular client who seems not to take any steps forward	My work with this client is wasted so I shouldn't spend much time with them
Scared	I have seen people be very aggressive in this situation	People are always aggressive here
Nervous	I didn't know what to say to someone in this situation	I will never know what to say when . . .
Sad	This made me think about my past and particular times when I have been very unhappy	I don't want to work in this situation as it will always make me feel sad
Sympathetic	This client really needs my help	I want to do things for them rather than help them to do things for themselves
Admiration	I am proud of this client	I expect too much of them
Indecisive	I never know which approach to take with this client	I will never 'get it right'
Excited	I like working with this client because I feel my work is worthwhile	I want the client to live up to my expectations of them rather than live their own life

circumstances in our professional practice, some ideas of the kinds of experiences that might prompt these and the assumptions we might make as a result in similar situations in the future. It is also important to remember that when we experience things we feel the feelings as well (see Chapter 6).

It is interesting to note that it is not only negative experiences that can lead us to make assumptions; positive ones can do this too. However, this does not mean that we should somehow try to set our feelings to one side, but rather that we should pay attention to them so that we can process them (Boud et al., 1985).

Reflective activity 7.3

Now think of some work, or personal situations that you have encountered, the feelings you had and the assumptions you then went on to make. You could do this in a table or just as notes.

Case study 7.2

Theo is training to be a nurse and is on placement in a learning disability assessment unit. He is finding the placement difficult and often goes home feeling drained physically and mentally. He regularly feels discouraged by the circumstances of the

(continued)

(continued)

patients, particularly the young adults. Some of the patients have very few visitors and some have none at all. Theo has a very supportive family and he is very close to his older brother. They have always supported one another and often speak of being best friends as well as brothers. Theo does not understand why some of the patients seem to be completely alone and he finds himself getting angry about this. He feels that parents should support their children no matter what, like his parents have always supported him, and that vulnerable people should not be left alone without the support of their family. He assumes that families who do not support their children are in the wrong and he cannot wait for his placement to end.

Argyris' Ladder of Inference

It is fair to say that each of us at some point in time has made assumptions, jumped to conclusions, which in turn have led to particular actions. In order to challenge our assumptions, we need to understand how assumptions are made – Argyris' (1982) Ladder of Inference is a very helpful explanation of this phenomenon. Figure 7.1 illustrates this.

Argyris argues that the Ladder of Inference works in this way. At the foot of the Ladder, we observe an event as it happens. Our human brains receive so many messages each day that we select the data we need or want at any given time. We then add meaning to that data, drawing on our current situation and our past experiences in similar situations. These meanings are drawn from the perspective of our own personal and cultural settings. From here we make assumptions and then draw conclusions about the person or the situation. These

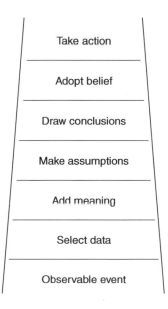

Figure 7.1 Argyris' Ladder of Inference

conclusions become part of our beliefs about the world and how it operates or, in other words, they become part of our worldview. The action we then take is based on our beliefs.

Once we reach this point we take one of two recursive loops (see Figure 7.2). The first loop is from our beliefs (the penultimate step on the Ladder) back to the second step on the Ladder where we automatically select data. In this loop, our beliefs lead us to make similar choices from our subsequent observations. In short, we most often select the data that supports our existing beliefs and ignore the data that might refute them; we see what we believe we see.

The second loop is from taking action at the very top of the Ladder to the bottom of the Ladder (see Figure 7.2). This involves taking action to seek more observable data. But this new data is also observed through the lens of our beliefs and these prompt us to notice what we have seen previously. Hence, our approach becomes biased in favour of our previous observations. Following either of these recursive loops means that our assumptions are strengthened and our existing beliefs are confirmed and even reinforced. So, in contrast to the well-known phrase 'I'll believe it when I see it', both loops prompt an 'I believe it, so I see it' approach.

Here is a very general example of how the Ladder of Inference operates.

A client you are working with behaves badly and you select data from what you observe. You only see their bad behaviour rather than anything good they might do or have done in the past. The meaning you add is that you are not surprised that they behave badly as in your experience many people you work with in this particular context behave like this. You then make assumptions about the person based on this, for example that this particular person is just like other people you meet here. From this you draw your own conclusions and come to believe that whenever you work in this particular setting, you will always deal with

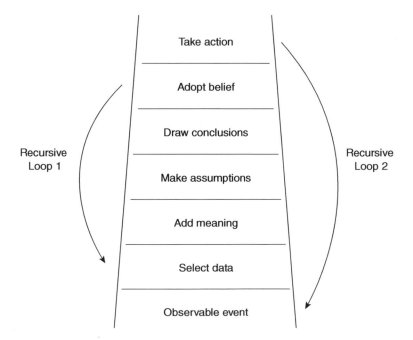

Figure 7.2 Argyris' Ladder of Inference and the recursive loops

difficult people. These beliefs then influence your actions in the future and you go into the situation expecting people to be difficult.

> Recursive loop 1 – based on the belief that everyone is difficult in this situation, you select data in the future and only see bad behaviour in the people you meet, thereby confirming your expectations.
>
> Recursive loop 2 – after taking action you then seek further observable data. But your data selection is based on your existing beliefs about how people behave here and again your expectations are confirmed.

Either way you see what you expect to see rather than what actually takes place and your assumptions have won the day. However, this can be avoided in two ways. First, we need to challenge our assumptions regularly by asking ourselves some questions such as:

- Do people always behave badly here or is it simply that this is what I am used to seeing?
- When did an individual last behave badly in this context?
- What might the reasons have been for their behaviour?
- Did I play any part in prompting their behaviour, for example, by being insensitive to their needs?

Second, we can actively seek out some contrary data that will disconfirm our assumptions. For example:

- Remind yourself that the context has been difficult in the past but that this does not mean that it will always be like this.
- Look for positives.
- Make a note of each time someone behaves well in this particular context.
- Make a note of anything you felt you did that helped towards a more positive atmosphere.

These are vital steps towards working in a non judgemental way.

Reflective activity 7.4

Now think about a situation where you feel you made some assumptions. How would you now be able to avoid the two recursive loops?

Case study 7.3

Megan is training to be a Maths teacher and is on placement in a secondary school. She dreads Friday afternoons because she has to teach the bottom set and the students can be uncooperative and difficult to manage. She has observed lots of bad behaviour and usually cannot wait for the lesson to end. Her mentor has become concerned

(continued)

(continued)

about her attitude to the class and asks her to think about some of the assumptions she is making. Emma soon realises that she expects very little of the students. The exercises and activities she chooses are often dull and do not demand very much from them. As a result, they get bored very easily and their behaviour deteriorates further. Megan decides to design more interesting and practical activities to try and engage the students more in the next lesson. She deliberately looks for any evidence of good behaviour and realises that many of the students behave well and in fact only a small number behave badly. She decides to discuss some specific strategies for working with the students who are not engaging with her lesson when she next sees her mentor.

Double loop learning (Argyris and Schön)

In Chapter 4 we examined Kolb's (1984) experiential learning cycle. This process involves having an experience that we later reflect on; this builds our knowledge and helps us as we prepare for the next experience. This kind of experiential learning is very valuable in professional practice and can be described as single loop learning (Argyris and Schön, 1974).

However, if we want to take our professional learning further and to engage with it at a deeper level, we need to challenge our established ways of thinking and of doing things, which in turn involves becoming aware of our assumptions. Critically reflective practice asks us to delve beneath the surface of our ideas to our beliefs and paradigms so that we can challenge our assumptions and, if necessary, adjust our habitual ways of viewing the world. In this regard Argyris and Schön's (1974) concept of double loop learning is very

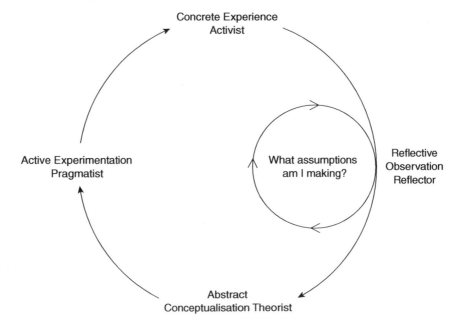

Figure 7.3 Double loop learning

useful (see Figure 7.3). Unlike Kolb's single loop cycle, double loop learning asks us to bring our assumptions to the surface and to question the things that we take for granted. This can lead us to explore further our personal values and beliefs that lie beneath our professional practice. Through this process, our perceptions and habits can change; we become more open minded and our practice can become more creative.

It is important to remember that exploring our assumptions is always challenging both personally and professionally. Taking a questioning approach can be helpful and here are some questions you could pose.

- Am I making any assumptions in this situation and if so, what are they?
- Are these assumptions valid?
- How would I justify them if I were asked to do so?
- Does this mean I am jumping to conclusions?
- Do my perceptions need to change?
- How does this affect my beliefs and how I see the world?

Such challenging can be done as part of the process of reflection following an experience as shown in Figure 7.4, but could be done during an experience too.

Reflective activity 7.5

Now think about an incident that happened recently where you felt you made some assumptions. What were they and how would you now respond to the questions posed above?

Case study 7.4

Tony is a newly qualified social worker and is working in a team providing care in the community for elderly clients. He regularly visits an 80-year-old who is being visited twice a day by carers to help him with his personal care. The client is keen to stay in his own home as long as possible as he values his independence. Whilst the client seems happy, Tony is concerned about the length of time he is spending on his own. He imagines that the client is lonely and that this could be bad for his mental health. He also thinks that it would be good if the client could get out of the house regularly and see something of the outside world. He tries to talk to the client about this, but the client assures him that as long as he has his regular visits from his carers, he is happy. He explains that one of them brings him his daily newspaper, which he loves to read and another always makes a cup of tea for both of them at the end of her visit and spends a few minutes chatting with him. Tony realises that he has assumed that the client is unhappy, when in fact he isn't. The client is happy in his own home and feels secure there. Tony begins to understand that the client sees the world differently from him and that the most important thing is that the client is happy.

Mezirow's seven levels of reflectivity that lead to 'perspective transformation'

In his work on transformative learning Mezirow (1978; 1981) puts forward descriptions of seven levels of reflectivity, which enable us to analyse how we approach people and situations. In particular, this helps us to think about assumptions we might be making in the light of past experiences. Reflectivity is often defined as the act of reflection, but, as indicated in Chapter 1, the terms reflection, reflectivity and reflexivity are sometimes used interchangeably, which can be confusing. The first four levels operate within our everyday consciousness, so are things that we are aware of on a regular basis – these include our feelings and personal values. The remaining three levels lie at a much deeper level and form part of our critical consciousness. At this level we become aware of the reasons why we sometimes make judgments about situations and people quickly, and in some cases why we can make these too quickly.

The seven levels are as follows:

1   Reflectivity – becoming aware of our view of things, people and situations. This also includes being aware of how we think and act in certain situations. So what do I think and feel about this person or situation and how does this affect how I behave?
2   Affective Reflectivity - not only becoming aware of our feelings in a particular situation, but also becoming aware of our feelings about how we think and act. So how do I feel about the way I think/act in these situations and am I comfortable with this?
3   Discriminant Reflectivity - questioning whether or not our perceptions about people are valid and accurate – are my perceptions correct?
4   Judgemental Reflectivity – involves becoming aware of our value judgements. These are often embedded within such things as our upbringing and can act as a guide to finding out more about our assumptions. So, what kind of value judgments might I be making?
5   Conceptual Reflectivity - questioning the constructs we use when we think about other people. So, why do I think of this person or these people in this particular way?
6   Psychic Reflectivity - recognising our prejudices and stereotypes that can make us quick to make judgements about people, often on the basis of limited information and even ignorance. So, am I just jumping to conclusions?
7   Theoretical Reflectivity – realising that the reason we make quick judgements about people is because these are based on our cultural and psychological assumptions. So, what are my assumptions about this person based on and in the light of this, should I be making such assumptions?

By exploring our thinking at each level, we can question our assumptions, in particular whether they are valid or not. This puts us in a stronger position to challenge our assumptions where we feel we cannot justify them and to reframe them where appropriate. Reaching the deepest level of Theoretical Reflectivity means that perspective transformation can happen. In other words, at this level I can begin to think about things differently.

Like many other theories, Mezirow's work has been criticised. In the same way as learning cycles can be critiqued by asking such questions as 'do things always happen in this particular sequence?', it is also legitimate to ask whether or not evidence for these levels can be found and whether the particular sequencing of them is accurate. In particular, Illeris (2014) argues that Mezirow's approach places too much emphasis on a cognitive, even logical process, which does not pay sufficient attention to the impact of feelings and values on professional practice. He argues that a holistic process of 'see – feel – change' enables us to challenge our assumptions rather than a purely rational one.

Equally, being aware of our assumptions does not then automatically imply that we take action to challenge them – as we know, taking action also involves choice. We cannot expect to be aware of our thinking at these seven levels on a daily basis, but they could give us some very useful insights into particularly challenging experiences or circumstances.

In his later work, Mezirow (2006) incorporates critical self-reflection of assumptions as a key aspect of perspective transformation. Also, by this time, he uses the helpful phrase 'habits of mind' to illustrate that our ways of thinking are often so ingrained that they have become habitual. Habits, as we know, can be very difficult to break, but not impossible. Positive habits of mind, including being open minded, seem particularly important in relation to learning and professional practice.

Reflective activity 7.6

Now think about areas of your work and development where it is particularly important to be open minded. How might you challenge your assumptions in these particular areas?

Case study 7.5

Julia is a counsellor who has been working with a woman for a number of months. In the recent past the woman has suffered from domestic violence by her estranged husband. Julia has worked hard to build a positive relationship with the client in a congruent and non-judgemental way, but she finds it very difficult when the client says that she still loves her husband, that he is now a reformed character and that she is thinking of living with him again. During the session, Julia begins to feel anxious and irritated by the client's apparent acceptance of her abusive husband. Following the session, Julia explores her feelings and the assumptions she thinks she might be making. She questions whether or not she is jumping to conclusions and whether her previous experiences of working with clients in situations like this means that she has just got into the habit of thinking 'this won't work'. Ultimately, she knows that the client is responsible for her own life, but decides that during the next session she will help the client to examine the advantages and disadvantages of living with her husband again. Julia hopes that this will help her to reflect on what she could gain and lose in her current situation.

A model for challenging limiting assumptions

When we think about the effect our assumptions have on our practice, it is easy to see that they can serve to restrict the way we view people and situations. If they are based on negative stereotypes this can be particularly detrimental and even damaging to clients. Challenging the assumptions we hold that limit the way we see things is an important element of learning and development and is a vital part of becoming and remaining an effective professional practitioner.

The Career Thinking Session (CTS) model (Bassot, 2015) offers a framework for challenging our limiting assumptions and can be used in supervision (see Chapter 9) or with a trusted colleague. It is a helpful approach to use when thinking about your career and professional development. The CTS itself involves intense listening (the term Listener is used for the person who carries out the session) to the person who wants to learn more about their career and professional development (the Thinker). The Listener poses the open question at the beginning of each step and then waits until the Thinker has finished saying all they wish to say, interjecting with statements such as 'that sounds interesting, tell me more about that' or 'I'm interested in why you said that. Can you please elaborate a bit more?' and so on.

Adapted from the work of Kline (1999) the CTS has the following six steps.

Step 1 – 'What do you want to think about?' Here, the Thinker expresses the thoughts and issues they have brought to the session. These might relate to things that the Thinker has found challenging in their professional practice, or something that has troubled them. Equally, it could be something that they feel very positive about that they would like to build upon. In Step 1 it is very important that the Listener does not rush in and move forward with the first idea or issue that the Thinker raises, as it is likely that anything raised initially might be (but will not always be) at a fairly superficial level of thinking. The Listener also needs to resist the temptation to try and solve the Thinker's problem or issue by offering advice or by moving too quickly to solutions. Such solutions are likely to come from the Listener's perspective and not from that of the Thinker and would probably result in little or no change. Once the Thinker has finished speaking and has nothing else to add, they are ready to move on to Step 2.

Step 2 – 'What do you want to achieve from the rest of the session?' This is an opportunity for the Thinker to express what they would like to focus on in the CTS. Again, it is important that the Listener waits for the Thinker to respond. Examples of many possible responses from Thinkers in relation to issues of career and professional development could include such things as 'to understand more about the difficulties I face in this area of my work', 'to understand more about why I find certain scenarios challenging', 'to explore how I can be more confident in my practice' or 'to think about adjusting my work-life balance'.

Step 3 – 'What are you assuming is stopping you from moving forward in your development?' This encourages the Thinker to begin to think about their limiting assumptions. Kline (1999) identifies three types of limiting assumptions: facts such as 'I don't have the relevant qualifications'; possible facts such as 'colleagues would not support me'; and bedrock assumptions about self and how life works, such as 'I'm not good enough' or 'I'm not talented enough'. Bedrock assumptions are deep rooted and will often (but not always) take time to come to the surface and can be likened to Brookfield's (1995) paradigmatic assumptions (see page 80). Often, they act as barriers to career and professional development and undermine someone's confidence and self-esteem. These assumptions are deep and develop over long periods of time, often from early childhood. They are so significant that they inform our beliefs and what we see as 'truth'. Reaching the bedrock assumption and articulating it is vital. In Step 3 the Thinker needs time to identify and articulate the bedrock assumption and may in some situations be reticent to do so. The Listener needs to recognise it and remember it.

Step 4 – 'If you knew that . . . what ideas would you have towards your development?' The ultimate goal in Step 4 is to enable the Listener to design the Incisive Question in relation to their bedrock assumption. As part of this process, the Thinker is asked to find the positive opposites to their limiting assumptions. Some of the positive opposites in relation to the examples used in *Step 3* could be, 'if you knew you could study to get the required qualifications' (fact), 'if you knew that your colleagues would support you' (possible fact), 'if you knew you were good enough' (bedrock) or 'if you knew you were talented enough' (bedrock). These questions encourage the Thinker to challenge their limiting assumptions by 'turning things on their head' and can help them to begin to think differently. It is important to emphasise that whilst the Listener can encourage the Thinker to pose relevant questions, the Thinker needs to articulate these questions in their own words. Limiting assumptions are particular to the individual concerned and are based on how they see the world, not how the Listener sees it. The Listener then asks the Thinker to identify the positive opposite to their bedrock assumption and to state this in relation to their further development. This is the Incisive Question (IQ), and is described as such because it cuts through the limiting bedrock assumption, serving to remove it, replacing it with a new, freeing assumption, which liberates the Thinker to think positively about their future. So, for example, the IQ for someone who says 'I am not talented enough' could be 'How can I best use my talents?' The IQ has cut through the limiting bedrock assumption, enabling the person to focus on their talents and to think about how they can use them.

Step 5 – Writing down the Incisive Question. The Incisive Question is very important and needs to be written down at the beginning of Step 5. Otherwise the danger is that it will be forgotten; the CTS could lose its focus and its positive impetus. Again, it must be written in the Thinker's own words. The Listener then asks the Incisive Question a number of times until the Thinker has voiced all their new positive ideas in relation to their future development.

Step 6 – Appreciation. This is unusual and could be unexpected for many in professional practice. We must always remember that sharing limiting assumptions is sensitive and challenging and demands trust and openness on both sides. Kline (1999) argues that the last step of appreciation keeps people thinking and asks both participants to share a positive quality they have found in each other and that they have valued during the session. This encourages the Thinker to continue to focus on the positives in relation to themselves and their future and to keep thinking past the session itself.

Reflective activity 7.7

What are your initial thoughts on the CTS model? Could the model be helpful, and if so, how? Is there someone that you could ask to help you to try it out?

Conclusion

In this chapter we have considered a range of issues related to assumptions. It is important to remember that challenging our own assumptions is rarely easy and can be uncomfortable. However, if we are seeking to evaluate our practice, doing this will form a vital part of our ongoing learning and development. In the next chapter we will focus on the role of feedback in this process.

References

Argyris, C. (1982) *Reasoning, Learning and Action: Individual and Organizational*, San Francisco: Jossey-Bass.

Argyris, C. and Schön, D. (1974) *Theory in Practice: Increasing Professional Effectiveness*, San Francisco: Jossey-Bass.

Bassot, B. (2015) 'The career thinking session: challenging limiting assumptions in career counselling', in M. McMahon and M. Watson (eds) *Career Assessment: Qualitative Approaches*, Rotterdam: Sense Publishers.

Boud, D., Keogh, R. and Walker, D. (1985) *Reflection: Turning Experience into Learning*, London: Routledge Falmer.

Brookfield, S.D. (1995) *Becoming a Critically Reflective Teacher*, San Francisco: Jossey-Bass.

Illeris, K. (2014). *Transformative Learning and Identity*, Abingdon: Routledge.

Kline, N. (1999). *Time to Think*, London: Ward Lock.

Kolb, D. (1984) *Experiential Learning: Experience as the Source of Learning and Development*, Upper Saddle River, NJ: Prentice Hall.

Mezirow, J. (1978) *Education for Perspective Transformation: Women's Reentry Programs in Community Colleges*, New York: Centre for Adult Education, Columbia University.

Mezirow, J. (1981) 'A critical theory of adult learning and education', *Adult Education*, 32(1), 13–24.

Mezirow, J. (2006) 'An overview on transformative learning' in P. Sutherland and J. Crowther (eds) *Lifelong Learning Concepts and Contexts*, Abingdon: Routledge.

Moss-Racusin, C.A., Dovidio, J.F., Brescoll, V.L., Graham, M.J. and Handelsman, J. (2012) 'Science faculty's subtle gender biases favour male students', in M. Wyer, M. Barbercheck, D. Cookmeyer, H.O. Ozturk and M. Wayne (eds) *Women Science and Technology: A Reader in Feminist Science Studies*, New York: Routledge, pp. 3–14.

8   The role of feedback in professional development

'There is no failure. Only feedback.'

(Robert Allen, 2012)

Introduction

In this chapter we will examine the vital role of feedback in professional development. We will begin by exploring the need for feedback and why this whole area can be problematic. The role of critical friendship will be discussed along with some strategies for finding some-one who will be able to carry out this role in a constructive way. This will be followed by an exploration of supervision, including some theoretical models that can help us to engage with this process to the benefit of our learning and development. The model of the Johari Window will then be introduced and the chapter will move on to look at the arguments of Eraut in relation to the important part feedback plays in critical reflection and professional effectiveness and the places where it can happen. The chapter will conclude with some final words on mentoring.

The need for feedback in professional development

It is important to consider why we need feedback and the role that it plays in our professional development. In Chapter 2 we explored the concept of the 'metaphorical mirror' and how we view our practice in different ways by looking into different kinds of mirrors. In particular, the ideas of using 'wing mirrors' to see things that are just out of our view and being aware that we can sometimes look at our practice using 'funfair mirrors' both serve as pointers to the need for feedback as a vital part of the process of enabling our professional development.

Reflective activity 8.1
Think of some specific areas where you feel that some feedback would be useful for your development.

So why is feedback so important? Here are some reasons:

- It stops us from just 'navel-gazing' which will limit our understanding of our practice.
- It prevents us from operating in some kind of vacuum.
- It helps us to see things from the perspectives of others, e.g. our colleagues, clients, managers.
- It challenges our critical thinking.
- It helps us to question our practice, including alternative approaches.
- It helps us to avoid complacency and feeling that our practice is 'good enough'.
- It prevents stagnation.
- It promotes creativity.
- It prompts deeper levels of thinking and analysis.
- It helps us to process our emotions.
- It helps us to challenge our assumptions.
- It keeps our practice 'sharp'.
- It is an opportunity for our practice to be affirmed by others.

Without feedback we risk the possibility of practising in some kind of 'bubble' or vacuum where we only see things from our own viewpoint. This can be limiting and in some cases even damaging. Being open to feedback is vital for professional development, but it is also important to understand that not all feedback is good feedback. Poor feedback is problematic; Table 8.1 shows characteristics of good feedback and contrasts this with poor feedback.

It is clear that good feedback enhances growth and professional development, and is constructive and supportive whilst being challenging at the same time. So how can we identify good feedback when we see or hear it? Table 8.2 details some words and phrases that can act as indicators of good and poor feedback.

Good feedback is given by people who listen a lot and talk a little. Their language is clear but somewhat tentative, often phrased as an open question so that the person can respond by putting across their view of events. So, 'How did you feel about this situation?' followed by 'Perhaps you could . . .' as distinct from 'That obviously went wrong didn't it?' followed by 'You need to do better next time by doing this'. Constructive feedback always includes development points to be considered for action – often, replacing the word 'but' with the word 'and' can make a big difference to how feedback is received. For example, 'I thought you handled the situation quite well but you should also have . . .' sounds negative and the person might not hear the suggestions, whereas 'I thought you handled the situation quite well and you could also consider . . .' is more positive whilst leaving the way open for the person to think about the possible suggestions.

It is always important to examine the feedback you receive and to assess its validity to help you to make decisions about the actions you feel you need to take. Here are some criteria you could use:

- Do you respect the person who is giving you feedback?
- Do they practice and behave in a way that inspires you?
- Do they have some kind of 'axe to grind'?

Table 8.1 Feedback

Good feedback is:	Poor feedback is:
Respectful	Disrespectful or even hurtful
Supportive	Damaging or accusatory
Encouraging	Discouraging
Honest	Brutally honest
Specific and focused	General
Clear	Vague or confusing
Timely	Delayed and given a long time after an event or too soon after a particularly difficult one
Not too much all at once	Too much to take in at any one time
Positive	Only negative, or accepts that everything is fine when it is not
Constructive with critique and development points, not simply positive	Destructive and lacking in critique
Helpful in identifying areas for development	Lacking any 'food for thought'
Done with a questioning approach	Done with a 'telling' approach
Motivating	De-motivating
Helpful in reaching new insights	Confusing and blurs new insights
Focused on professional issues	Mainly focused on personal issues
Spoken adult to adult	Patronising or condescending
Done by posing questions	Done by seeking to give answers or solutions
Fair	Biased
Tentative	Curt
Based on clear evidence	Based on hearsay

Table 8.2 Good and bad feedback

Words and phrases used in good feedback	Words and phrases used in poor feedback
. . . and . . .	. . . but . . .
You could think about . . .	It has to be said that you need to . . .
Here are some things that you could consider . . .	You are a grown up so here's the thing . . .
What do you feel you need to work on?	You really need to improve . . .
Sometimes . . ., often . . .	Always . . ., never . . .
It appears to me that . . .	You . . .
Who . . ., what . . ., where . . .	Why (on earth) . . .?
What would you do if . . .?	Why didn't you just . . .?
As well as	Instead of

- Do they have your development interests at heart?
- Do they have their own agenda?
- Are they open to feedback themselves?

Reflective activity 8.2

Now think of times when you have received some feedback. How would you describe the quality of the feedback and why?

Case study 8.1

Shirley is training to be a nurse and is finding her placement on a medical ward difficult. She is working closely with a qualified nurse, but finds that she is very critical of everything Shirley does. Shirley feels that she is continually being told off and it gets to the point where she feels that she can't do anything right. During a particularly difficult shift, Shirley becomes upset when the nurse speaks to her in a very offhand way. Later, one of the patients seems upset and says to Shirley 'she shouldn't speak to you like that'. The following day Shirley decides to ask the nurse at the beginning of the shift if she can give her some feedback on the things she is doing well as well as all the mistakes she is making. The nurse is surprised and says 'No one ever gives me any positive feedback, that's why I get so discouraged'. Shirley and the nurse decide that they will give one another at least one positive feedback point each day when they do something well. This helps Shirley to build a much more positive relationship with the nurse and the placement becomes easier.

One model for structuring feedback is called the 'praise sandwich'. This begins with some positives, then the focus moves to some areas for development or things that could be improved and finishes with a summary of the positives. It is always important to remember that it is very difficult for someone to move forward in their development if they only ever receive negative messages; everyone needs positive things to build on.

Feedback given in the form of the 'praise sandwich' can boost confidence, build someone's self esteem and helps them to see where they could improve. It is fair to say that confidence is a very delicate and intangible thing – difficult to gain and very easy to undermine or even destroy. It is always worth remembering this whenever you are giving or receiving feedback.

The 'praise sandwich' is not without its critics, of course. For example, its use can become obvious and as a result people can either focus on the positive and forget the criticism, or do the opposite and focus only on the praise and fail to hear any development points. If too much praise is given with too little emphasis on development, people can get the idea that everything was fine when this might not be the case. This is an easy trap to fall into if you need to give some challenging feedback to someone at any point, as it is always much easier to say positive things. If too little praise is given, the praise can be seen as tokenistic and appear superficial or even insincere, and is likely to be ignored. Feedback that involves praise followed by development points using words like 'as well as' and 'you could develop this by . . .' and concluding with more praise is supportive, constructive and developmental.

One final point to remember is that body language is important too, both on the part of the person who is giving feedback and for the person receiving it. Keeping your body language open will ensure that communication flows effectively both ways, and avoiding things like folding your arms and crossing your legs will show that you are ready to listen and are open to what is being said.

Case study 8.2

Tracey is training to be an English teacher and is interested in working with students with challenging behaviour. She is doing a placement in an inclusion unit in a large secondary school. At the end of each day staff in the unit meet together for a debriefing session; they discuss things that have happened during the day, how situations were handled and what can be learned for the future. Tracey finds these sessions very helpful and can see the 'praise sandwich' being used effectively. She realises that staff are very good at being aware of what they do well. She also notices that people spend time discussing the challenging situations they have had to deal with during the day and people are keen to hear about alternative approaches that could have worked more effectively. Towards the end of the session, the Inclusion Manager asks each person to share their highlight of the day and the meeting always ends on a very positive note. Sharing different approaches that are working well helps everyone to feel that they are succeeding in their practice and overall most members of staff are well motivated in spite of the very challenging students they are working with.

The role of critical friendship

Some programmes of professional training ask people to work with a critical friend as part of their learning and development. A critical friend is someone who will help you to engage with many aspects of your development, particularly in relation to self-awareness. Working with a critical friend will help you to give and receive valuable feedback on your practice and it will be important to choose a critical friend carefully. As a term, critical friendship can appear as a contradiction in terms in that a friend would not usually be defined as someone who is critical. However, it is a true friend who will sensitively point out where we might be going wrong – someone who will let us know tactfully that we have ice cream round our mouth or broccoli in our teeth!

A good critical friend is someone who you know and can trust and who puts you at ease. They are a good listener and someone who is not afraid to pose questions in a sensitive but challenging way. They act with integrity and you can rely on them to keep the issues you discuss confidential. They are positive, encouraging and always constructive. They do not shy away from negatives or areas for development and offer critique rather than negative criticism.

The core qualities of critical friendship are as follows:

- Mutual respect.
- Trust.
- Openness.
- Honesty.
- A good relationship and rapport.
- Unconditional positive regard (Rogers, 1951).

One vital aspect of effective critical friendship is a sensitive and questioning approach. It is not the role of a critical friend to be negative or destructive, but to sensitively offer critique to help their friend to examine their approach and actions in particular situations. Using open questions that begin with 'what', 'when' and 'where' are good places to start as they give the other person the opportunity to speak freely, for example, 'What made you respond in that way in that particular situation?' Hypothetical questions can be especially useful, such as 'How would you feel if you were the client?' and 'If this had happened in a different setting how might you have responded?' These can help someone to see things from a different perspective.

Critical friendship can be a very effective way of giving and receiving feedback that can enhance our learning and development. It is important to spend some time thinking about who your critical friend could be and it is worth remembering that it might not be your best friend. It will be someone upon whom you can rely to be open and honest. They may not always say what you want to hear and ultimately this will be more valuable than working with someone who finds it difficult to help you to probe the more challenging aspects of your practice.

Case study 8.3

Roger is training to be a Careers Adviser and as part of his reflective practice module he is asked to work with a critical friend. The tutor is clear that in order to help clients with their career decisions it is vital that Careers Advisers have high levels of self-awareness, particularly in relation to any prejudices they might have, which can cause them to stereotype people and thereby restrict clients' aspirations. Roger asks one of his fellow students to be his critical friend because he knows he can trust him and feels that they can both be honest with one another without being harsh. During their course their critical friendship helps Roger to consider some significant issues, particularly in relation to his fears of working with clients with disabilities. His critical friend asks what experience he has had with people with disabilities and Roger soon realises that many of his fears come from being very inexperienced in this area. Roger's critical friend encourages him to visit a local special school as part of his placement activity and offers to discuss it with him afterwards. During the discussion they focus on what Roger has learned and how his views have changed. As a result Roger feels more confident about the possibility of working with students with additional needs in mainstream schools in the future.

The role of supervision

In some professional areas (for example counselling, social work) supervision is seen as important for two reasons. First, it enables practitioners to reflect on their practice in a regular and deep way by helping them to view things from a number of different perspectives. Second, it protects the client from practice that might not be in their best interest or could even be oppressive and damaging. Bearing in mind some of the sensitive and extremely challenging situations that, for example, a social worker might face, the idea of a safe space where practice can be discussed openly and in detail is vital in helping practitioners who find themselves faced with the evitable question, 'Did I do the right thing?'. This is particularly the case when there is no single 'right thing' to do, but only multiple actions that could justifiably be taken.

The term supervision is a difficult one to define because this varies depending on the particular professional context. If you have access to supervision, it will be important to check the meaning of supervision within your particular work setting. This kind of supervision should not be confused with performance related supervision usually provided by a line manager. This focuses on the achievement (or otherwise) of goals and targets that have been set beforehand. One somewhat thorny issue raised within the literature of supervision is whether or not it should be done by a line manager, or whether this restricts what can then be easily discussed. Some professions would argue that this kind of supervision should be carried out by someone not involved, even by someone outside the organisation if possible. Others would argue that it can be helpful to have a manager's perspective. In many circumstances there is simply no choice.

It is also important to understand that supervision is not always open to everyone who feels they need it or could benefit from it. In the early days of a new job, it is good to check out the possible opportunities for supervision and to consider making use of them wherever possible.

Like feedback, we cannot assume that all supervision is good supervision. Good supervisors often have many of the qualities of good teachers and good practitioners and show many of the characteristics discussed earlier in relation to good feedback. They show respect for their supervisee and demonstrate empathy. They take a questioning approach as distinct from a didactic or directive one and have finely tuned listening skills. A sense of humour is important too on both sides. It is worth remembering that supervisors need good feedback too, and this can help to build and maintain a healthy working relationship.

There are several theoretical models that explain the concept of supervision and one of the most well known is that of Proctor (1986). Proctor uses the following three terms to describe the purpose of supervision.

> *Normative* – this involves monitoring the work of the practitioner to make sure that they are practicing effectively, competently and ethically. This includes checking that the relevant code of practice is being applied consistently and appropriately. The main question being asked from this perspective is 'Is the practitioner meeting the norms of their particular profession?'

Formative – the focus here is on professional development and the aim is to help the practitioner to develop their skills, professional knowledge and appropriate attitudes and values. This leads to a greater and deeper level of reflection and self-awareness. The main question being asked here is 'How can this practitioner develop themselves further?'

Restorative – this is sometimes referred to as supportive and is concerned with the support practitioners need when facing challenging situations. Such situations can cause stress and sometimes distress and it is important that practitioners have the opportunity to process their emotional responses (see Chapter 6). The main question being asked here is 'How can this practitioner be supported in these challenging situations?'

Effective supervision can only happen in a safe space and supervisors and supervisees both have a responsibility to ensure that it can take place effectively. The following points are worth bearing in mind:

- The setting for supervision is important. It should be comfortable, private and away from interruptions.
- A high level of trust between supervisor and supervisee needs to be built.
- The discussion is confidential – nothing is disclosed to another party without the permission of the discloser and only if they or their client are at risk of harm or are violating the law. Specific details of clients do not need to be shared to avoid bias and preconceptions.
- Be clear about why supervision is needed and who has asked for it to take place.
- Set aside some specific time and keep it free.
- Be mindful of the seating arrangements – easy chairs at the same height around a low table conveys a more relaxed equal discussion.
- Both supervisor and supervisee should spend time preparing for the session, thinking about what they wish to discuss and gain from the session. Time is precious and time spent in supervision should be time invested in professional development.
- In an initial session be sure to agree some 'ground rules' regarding what will and will not take place during supervision. These can provide some helpful boundaries to the supervisory relationship.
- Always be sure to follow up any action that you agreed to take in the previous session.
- Be prepared to be open and to reflect at a deep level about such things as your emotions, attitudes, beliefs and values.
- Be appreciative of one another – appreciation keeps people thinking.

Case study 8.4

Shakira is training to be a social worker and has regular supervision as part of her course, which she finds very helpful. Shakira has built up a good relationship with her supervisor, who helps her to examine a wide range of issues regarding her work placements, particularly when she finds situations troubling. During the early days of meeting with her supervisor, Shakira often used the sessions to offload how she was feeling, which helped her to become less anxious about her work and to feel supported.

(continued)

(continued)

After a while, Shakira recognised that she wanted to begin to develop her practice further and began to ask her supervisor to discuss specific situations that she was finding challenging at the time. This helped Shakira to see those aspects of her practice where she was becoming competent and those where she needed to do more work. From this, she was able to devise an informal action plan for her further development.

Reid and Westergaard (2013) argue that supervision is a parallel process. This means that the interpersonal skills used in professional practice (like empathy, congruence or genuineness and active listening) are mirrored in the supervision session by both people. Supervision is often recognised as an important process for people in the helping professions because it enriches practice and reduces stress.

Johari Window

The Johari Window was developed by Joseph Luft and Harry Ingham and is a model that can help us to gain some useful insights into how we relate to other people; this can give us greater self-awareness regarding how we communicate with others both individually and in groups.

The Johari Window is a square-shaped window with the following four panes:

1   Top left – the Open area, sometimes called the Arena. This includes the things we know about ourselves and the things others know about us. This includes such things as our skills, knowledge and behaviour, which together form our 'public history'.

2   Top right – the Blind area. This contains things that we do not know about ourselves but that others know, and things that we cannot see about ourselves but that others sometimes can. This can include simple facts, but also other more intangible and deeper things. For example, we may lack confidence in certain areas which others may be able to see, but that we cannot. We may lack self esteem and feel inadequate, but cannot always see this ourselves.

3   Bottom left – the Hidden area. This includes the things we know about ourselves but that others do not know about us. In any professional context it is important to remember that the things we disclose with others will have valid limits to them. For example, we will usually disclose more of ourselves to family and friends than to colleagues and clients.

4   Bottom right – the Unknown area. This contains all the things that we do not know about ourselves and that others do not know.

The model shows how feedback (Ask – running across the top of the square) and self-disclosure (Tell – running up and down the vertical side of the square) can help us to gain greater self-awareness. In general terms, in order to know ourselves better, we need a larger Open pane in the top left of the square. This can be achieved in two ways. First, we can ask for feedback from others, which moves the vertical line in the middle of the window across to the right, reducing our Blind area in the right hand corner. In addition, we can tell others more about ourselves, thereby moving the horizontal line down and making our Hidden area smaller.

In particular, being open to receiving feedback from others and engaging with it enables us to become more aware of things that others know about us and see in us, but that we do not necessarily see in ourselves. This is particularly helpful in relation to learning about ourselves at a deeper level. Good feedback can build confidence and self esteem. Similarly, being willing to disclose to others will enable them to get to know us better and will encourage open two-way communication.

All professionals need to be open to feedback for their professional growth and development. In addition, the Johari Window model can help us in our professional relationships with those we are supporting. For example, the right amount of self-disclosure at the right time can build empathy. But it is important to remember that in any professional situation, whether in a feedback situation with a colleague or client, self-disclosure always involves a choice and you should never disclose something unless you are comfortable doing so. Indeed, in some professional settings, self-disclosure can be seen as problematic, as it could distract from the needs of the person you are supporting. So self-disclose should only be done with caution and care.

Case study 8.5

Richard is a podiatrist who enjoys building good working relationships with his clients, some of whom he sees regularly over a period of time. Richard is keen to get feedback from his clients as he finds it helps him to meet his clients' needs more effectively. Working with one particular client has become difficult recently as the woman concerned no longer seems to want to talk to him very much during their sessions. Richard decides to ask her for some feedback to see if there is anything he can do to restore her trust. The client says that she sometimes finds the sessions painful and feels that at times he can be a bit heavy handed. As a result she has started to dread coming to the sessions and cannot wait for them to be over. Until now Richard has had no idea of this; he thanks the client for her feedback and explains how valuable her feedback is in enabling him to give the best possible care. He also talks to her about appropriate pain relief.

As discussed previously, giving and receiving feedback always involves an element of risk taking, so an atmosphere of trust is vital. It is well worth remembering that it is possible to be too open and to disclose too much. In professional practice it is right that some things remain in the Hidden area. Some things are disclosed more appropriately only in supervision or with a more experienced colleague and others only with family or close friends.

Eraut on feedback

Having established that feedback is an important vehicle for professional development, Eraut (2006), writing in the context of education management, usefully describes four different settings where feedback can occur. They are as follows:

- Immediate and in situ – this is feedback that is given during or immediately following an event and is given by a colleague or someone who witnesses it. It is usually specific and focuses on the factors that had an impact on the particular situation, which can easily be forgotten later.
- Informal conversations away from the workplace or place of study – feedback here can be planned or unplanned and relies on the learning culture with the given context.
- Mentoring and supervision – here, feedback is more formal and can also be related to performance (Eraut uses the word supervision here in the management sense of the word). The mentor or supervisor will not necessarily have direct opportunities to observe the work they have to supervise.
- Appraisal – this is more formal and less frequent feedback, which relates to the achievement of goals and objectives set previously.

Eraut is clear that receiving feedback will not always be easy and may not be a positive experience. At times it can even be distressing. But unless we are open to it we can fool ourselves into thinking that 'I did the best I could in the circumstances' or 'I must have misunderstood what was required. If things had been clearer, I would have known what to do'. He also points to the need to process feedback and to take appropriate action on it, rather than passively receiving it. Again, this highlights the issue of choice; listening, taking some time to process the feedback and acting upon it when we feel it is justified and appropriate always involves making decisions. This could alter our perspectives and help us to begin to see ourselves and the situations we encounter differently.

Some final words about mentoring

The value of mentoring newly qualified teachers is very well known and widely researched (Heikkinen, Jokinen and Tynjälä, 2012). This often involves an ongoing relationship with someone you trust and respect and can be an excellent way of helping you to develop your practice further. In relation to mentoring, the phrase 'Get One and Be One' is useful to remember; people in all walks of life can benefit from support from experienced colleagues, whilst experienced practitioners can also learn from the enthusiasm and ideas of people who are new to a profession. Your developing skills of facilitation and communication will equip you to be a mentor to others even if you might not have lots of experience at the moment.

Conclusion

In this chapter we have explored several aspects of the vital role of feedback in professional development. We have discussed what characterises good and poor feedback and the role of critical friendship. The value of supervision was explored and the model of the Johari Window presented. The chapter concluded with some insights from the work of Eraut and some final thoughts on mentoring. In the next chapter we will focus on reflecting in groups.

References

Allen, Robert (2012) *No Such Things as Failure*, NLP World. Available from http://www.nlpworld.co.uk/no-such-thing-as-failure/. Accessed 7 May 2015.

Eraut, M. (2006) 'Feedback' in *Learning in Health and Social Care*, 5(3): 111–118.

Heikkinen, H.L.T., Jokinen, H and Tynjälä, P. (2012) *Peer-Group Mentoring for Teacher Development*, Abingdon: Routledge.

Luft, H. (1984) *Group Processes: An Introduction to Group Dynamics*, Mountain View, CA: Mayfield.

Proctor, B. (1986) 'Supervision: a co-operative exercise in accountability' in A. Marken and M. Payne (eds) *Enabling and Ensuring: Supervision in Practice*, Leicester: Leicester National Youth Bureau/Council for Education and Training in Youth and Community Work.

Reid, H.L. and Westergaard, J. (2013) *Effective Supervision for Counsellors: An Introduction*, Exeter: Learning Matters.

Rogers, C. (1951) *Client-Centred Therapy*, London: Constable.

9 Reflecting in groups

'And time for reflection with colleagues is for me a lifesaver; it is not just a nice thing to do if you have the time. It is the only way you can survive.'

(Margaret J. Wheatley, 2012)

Introduction

In this chapter we will explore the area of reflecting with others in groups. If reflection is purely a solitary activity we can become immersed in our own point of view, seeing things only from our perspective, which inevitably is narrow, limited and even biased. Reflecting with others enables us to gain insights from them and to question our thoughts and actions in the light of these. The chapter begins with a discussion in order to define what a group is and how the term will be used. The different types of groups we might encounter in professional practice will then be identified and the benefits of reflecting in groups will be discussed. Some key principles of effective group facilitation will then be explored and the importance of 'ground rules' and a positive environment emphasised. The dangers and difficulties of reflecting in groups will then be considered with some pointers for overcoming them. This will be followed by a series of exercises that can be carried out in groups in order to promote critical reflection.

What is a group?

On the surface this seems to be a simple question, but it might be more complex than it first appears. In addition, the terms group and team can be used in literature to mean the same thing, which can be confusing. The term group suggests that more than two people are involved and that they have some kind of common purpose. This is also the case for a team, but being involved in a team usually implies that individuals have a certain role or roles to play. A simple example to illustrate this point is that a sports team cannot succeed if every player wants to play in the same position. A team is organised in a particular way to enable it to achieve its goals, whereas a group is more fluid and flexible in nature. Forsyth (2006: 2-3) defines a group as 'two or more individuals who are connected to one another by social relationships'.

In this chapter the term group is used to mean a collective of people, usually three or more, who are connected by a common purpose. In this case the purpose is to critically reflect on practice. Groups of this kind often have between five and eight members; a group of more than eight can have a tendency to begin to split into two as some individuals might feel that they do not have enough space to talk and others might feel less comfortable speaking with a large number of people present. Two people meeting together would be described as a dyad or critical friendship as discussed in Chapter 8.

Types of group

Different professions have different kinds of groups to help practitioners to reflect on their practice and to critically evaluate the work they are doing with clients. Some of these are as follows.

Peer support groups

These offer a space for practitioners to meet as equals and discuss their practice. They tend to be fairly informal and are not necessarily led by one particular member. Members come along with ideas of what they want to discuss with colleagues and are given time and space to put their views forward while group members listen and offer insights but without offering solutions. The atmosphere is one of listening and reciprocal support. Peer support is also used in schools, where students are trained to support one another in order to alleviate stress (Cowie and Wallace, 2000).

Action learning sets

Often used in the area of leadership development, the focus of action learning sets is on problem solving and these can be a very useful way of developing practice, particularly if there are difficulties identified in specific areas (Revans, 2011). Action learning is built on the relationship between reflection and action; time in the action learning set is given over to questioning and critical reflection and identifying action to follow. In an action learning set a small group of practitioners meets together to analyse the issues and problems that the individuals bring and each group member is given time to air their views and explain their problem. The group helps each person to consider a range of perspectives in relation to the problem and action is then planned with the structured support of the group. The group is responsible for the selection of the topic(s) and/or problem(s) discussed which are real rather than hypothetical, and this can be an effective group method for reflecting on experience. Action learning sets function well in an atmosphere of trust, friendship and support where members can feel safe to express their concerns freely.

Triads

A triad is a group of three people who meet together to discuss their learning and development and also to practice a range of different interpersonal skills. Triads can involve role play of different situations or scenarios with one person acting as the practitioner, another the role of the client, whilst the third person acts as an observer who leads discussion and feedback on what has taken place following the activity. The use of triads is common in the training of counsellors (Bager-Charleson, 2010), but can also be a useful approach for people in other professions. The scenarios can be taken as examples from practice or can be hypothetical.

Guided reflection groups

This is a small group of student practitioners (approximately 10) who meet together regularly and are facilitated by a mentor (Johns, 2013). Each student brings along at least two experiences that they have reflected on – one positive and self-affirming and one problematic (see Chapter 5). They refer to relevant theory as appropriate and the students keep an ongoing reflective journal. The mentor facilitates a space for curiosity and reflection so that the students can build their confidence and find their own way through the situations they are facing.

Group supervision

The area of supervision was discussed in Chapter 8, where the focus was on one to one meetings with a supervisor. Supervision can also be done effectively in small groups led by an experienced practitioner, when the same models can be applied.

Reflective activity 9.1

How helpful would you find reflecting with others in a group? If so, how? Is there a group that you could join?

Case study 9.1

Sophie works in the international office in a university and she is undertaking a leadership programme. As part of the programme she is part of an action learning set which meets to discuss issues relevant for people in the group. At the meeting, each person is allocated 30 minutes; during the first five minutes the person describes what they want to discuss and for the following 25 minutes, group members pose open questions to help the person to think things through at a deeper level. Sophie decides that she would like to discuss the possibilities for her future and whether or not she should stay in her current job or move to a new one. The group members ask Sophie a number of open questions, such as 'What do you enjoy about your current job?', 'What do you dislike?' and 'How would you like to develop in the future?' During the discussion Sophie begins to see that she does not find her job as satisfying as she used to and, in particular, that she now finds all the travelling she has to do very draining. She realises that she needs to give much more thought to her future in order to examine her options more carefully. She plans to discuss her development with her manager, update her CV and start to search for job vacancies on two key websites to see what is available. She asks people in the group if they could meet again in a month's time to discuss her progress.

The benefits of reflecting in groups

Reflecting in groups has many benefits and, often, practitioners welcome the opportunity to discuss their practice in some depth with their colleagues. Discussion develops our understandings, and having a supportive space to explain and explore aspects of practice with colleagues helps us to sharpen our thinking and critique our ways of working. Reflecting with others can be useful for the following reasons.

It prevents isolation

The work of some practitioners is relatively isolated. For example, a teacher in her classroom, a counsellor in his counselling room, a school nurse in her clinic or a social worker visiting families may spend much of their time working alone albeit with their clients. Some may then return to an office or centre where they have contact with colleagues whilst others might work more independently from home. In such circumstances it is easy to feel isolated and for professional practice to become blinkered. The opportunity to reflect with colleagues in a group can prevent feelings of isolation.

It prevents burn out

Meeting with others and sharing experiences gives us the opportunity to 'offload' and to externalise our thoughts and feelings. Without this we risk the possibility of only looking inwardly, which, for some, can lead to mental exhaustion and even burn out.

It offers different perspectives

Perhaps most importantly, reflecting with others gives us the chance to see our practice from different perspectives. Each individual client and practitioner is different and discussion helps us to gain valuable insights from others into what we did and why, how things worked or otherwise and how we might be able to approach things differently to greater effect.

It develops our understanding of practice

Professional practice is constantly changing, and discussing a range of issues with other professionals (if possible with those outside our own profession as well as those within it) can help us to gain new understandings of effective work in supporting people.

It helps us to be creative

Gaining new understandings can lead to creativity in our practice as we try out new ideas and approaches in our work. These can then be discussed with others following their implementation.

It prevents stagnation

Without discussion our practice can become stale and we risk operating on 'autopilot'. We can become bored and ultimately could stagnate; this is bad for us and bad for our clients too.

It helps us to process our emotions

In Chapter 6 we explored how professional practice prompts an emotional response and showed us that we all need opportunities to process our feelings. Many practitioners find discussion helpful as part of this. As individuals we can be 'tied up' in our own emotions, particularly when we experience difficult situations and are trying to support challenging people. In such circumstances other people can often offer a more objective perspective; they will not have such an emotional response because they were not personally involved in the situation. In addition, their perspectives will be different because they are individuals who have had different experiences from us and have different memories of their past. All of this means that they can be more objective than we can about the situation. However, we must always remember that because of their own previous experiences, no one can be completely objective.

It helps us to question our assumptions

In Chapter 7 we examined the whole area of assumptions in professional practice. Discussing these can be challenging but plays a vital part when working in an anti discriminatory way.

It helps us cope with stress

To say that professional practice is stressful seems like an understatement. We all need strategies to help us to cope with stress as practice becomes more and more demanding, and discussion with colleagues can be one such strategy.

Reflective activity 9.2

For you, what are, or would be, the main benefits of reflecting in a group?

Facilitating effective groups

In order for a group to work effectively it needs to be facilitated well, otherwise it is likely that conversations will be lengthy, albeit very interesting and often stimulating. People who work with people usually like discussing their practice at length! Unfortunately, this can mean that the focus and direction of the discussion is quickly lost as group members become immersed in detail, comparing their own practice with that of others in the group. Discussions can become very protracted as group members remember things that they have experienced and phrases like 'That also happened to me when . . .', 'I know what you mean,

Table 9.1 Key differences between facilitation and leadership

A group facilitator	A group leader
Works with a group in a non hierarchical way	Takes a leadership role which involves or at least implies a hierarchical relationship
Works with group members on an equal basis	Is aware of issues of power, authority and control and may need to ask participants to carry out certain specific tasks
Is focused on the group process	Is focused on outcomes and the achievement of objectives as well as on the process
Asks group members to negotiate and agree what will be discussed in a group session	Sets an agenda for meetings and circulates this beforehand
Is a neutral mediator who does not offer their opinions or solutions	Works towards solutions and offers their own views on how these can be reached
Poses questions to help the group members to think at a deeper level	Poses questions to help the group to examine different options in order to reach conclusions to make progress toward objectives

when that happened to me I . . .', and so on can regularly be heard. The role of the facilitator is to work with the group to keep it 'on track' and to ensure that the group works effectively to achieve its purpose.

At this point it is important to understand the difference between the terms facilitator and leader in the context of working in a group. A phrase that is often used to describe this difference is that leadership is done to a group and facilitation is done with a group. Whilst leaders also need to be good facilitators, facilitators are not asked to take a leadership role. Table 9.1 highlights some of the key differences between facilitation and leadership.

Facilitating a group effectively is a highly skilled task and, therefore, is most often done by experienced practitioners. However, when this is not possible (which can often be the case in busy professional practice), less experienced people need to be ready to take on this role from time to time. So it is important not to be taken by surprise if you find yourself in a situation where you need to facilitate a group, even if only occasionally. You will be able to use many of the interpersonal skills you are learning in your professional practice as they are eminently transferable into this role (Culley and Bond, 2011; Thompson, 2011). Like many other areas of professional practice, the skills of group facilitation are best learned through experience.

Here are some important aspects to bear in mind when facilitating groups:

- You are not an expert. Remember that your primary role is to enable the discussion to keep its focus and to guide effective communication. If something comes up in discussion and people look to you for an answer, ask the group members for their views. In all instances, be honest about the limitations of your knowledge. If there is something you do not know, say so, and ask the group to do some research on this afterwards rather than offering to do this for them. This hands power and control over to the group and promotes group learning.

- At all times resist the temptation to push your own agenda or to offer advice. This will only discourage people from speaking and will subsequently close the discussion down. Before you know it, the focus of the group will be on you, which will not help group members to reflect on their own practice.

- Work towards an atmosphere of trust. Trust is intangible and is difficult to build and therefore takes time to foster and maintain. By contrast, it can be destroyed in minutes or even seconds. It is important to welcome comments and observations, particularly if someone is new to a group. Be positive about all contributions (particularly when it is clear that these have been difficult or sensitive to make) and never 'put anyone down'. Comments such as 'Thank you for sharing that with us' and 'That must have been very difficult for you' can go a long way to affirm people and to encourage them to continue to be open, which will help communication to flow.

- If a group is new, it is very helpful to set some 'ground rules' during an early meeting in order to be clear about what is expected within the group. This is best achieved through discussion where group members are involved in deciding how they would like to work together. This could cover such issues as where the group will meet, at what time and for how long. It is good to include a discussion on issues of confidentiality, respecting one another's views and trust, as well as such things as listening and not talking over one another. The facilitator should make a record of the ground rules and suggest that the group returns to them if any difficulties are experienced. In addition, it is usually helpful to review the ground rules periodically to make sure that they continue to be fit for purpose.

- Be aware that disclosure in a group always involves taking a bigger risk than sharing something in a pair or with your critical friend. This means that it will take time for people to reach the point where they feel safe and confident enough to disclose things about themselves and their practice. In the early days of a group consider asking people to take part in some warm up activities to help them to get to know one another better. Be sure to have breaks so that people have an informal opportunity to speak to one another to build their relationships.

- It is important to consider the location of group meetings; if at all possible it must be convenient for all group members and if this is difficult (for example, if group members work at some distance from one another) consider rotating the venue in order to be fair to everyone. A suitable room will be needed that is comfortable, with easy chairs all at the same height and with facilities for hot and cold drinks. Whilst this might sound like basic etiquette, it is surprising what a difference such things can make to effective communication.

- Be ready to challenge contributions in a positive way in order to encourage everyone to think at a deeper level. Sensitive challenging is done best by posing a tentative open question, such as 'I'm interested in . . . What made you say that in particular?' and 'How might you want to respond to that situation now?' These can help people to think at a deeper level and challenge themselves. This is often much more effective than being challenged by others via comments such as 'If I were you . . .'

- Listen, listen and listen some more. The importance of listening cannot be over emphasised and it can be very tiring! Unless you listen attentively to each contribution, you will not be able to reflect on what people are saying and pose questions to make them think more. You will also miss important things that people are sharing.

- Show people that you are listening through your body language. Open body language (for example, being careful not to fold your arms) shows that you are open to hear what people have to say. In turn, they are likely to then mirror this in their body language and communication will flow more effectively.
- Maintain some eye contact with group members. The key here is not too much and not too little.
- Consider having an observer: someone who will observe the group and give feedback on how people are communicating with each other. This role can be rotated effectively so that each group member takes a turn in observing the group and then giving feedback.
- Be a people watcher. You might notice that one or more group members keep their body language closed, for example by crossing their legs. It might be difficult to have any eye contact with them and communication might be rare and sparse. In such instances it is usually best to speak to them individually after the session, again by posing a tentative question like 'I couldn't help but notice today that you seemed uncomfortable. Is this something you would like to talk about?' Of course, the individual has the right to say no and this should always be respected.
- At all times remember to consider any relevant ethical dimensions, particularly regarding any disclosures of unprofessional behaviour and how these will be addressed. The identity and details of all clients needs to remain anonymous.
- Remember that everyone can learn and that nobody is perfect, including you. Group facilitation is a difficult task, so do not be discouraged if you feel you have got some things wrong. It is rare indeed for someone to get everything right as none of us are perfect.

Case study 9.2

Chen is a learning mentor in a primary school who has recently completed a degree in supporting children and young people. Through the course he has got to know several learning mentors from different local schools. Now that the course has finished, some of the students suggest meeting together each term to discuss their practice. Chen is keen to do this and has always got on very well with everyone. As a result, several members of the group have asked if he will facilitate the group. Chen explains that he has never done this kind of thing before, but that he is prepared to have a go and see how he gets on. Before the meeting, Chen asks everyone about a location for the group and they decide to meet in a different school each time to make things fair for everyone. Chen asks the host of the first meeting to arrange for a room with easy chairs and to arrange for hot drinks and water to be available. During the first meeting, Chen asks the group to discuss how they want to work together and agree some ground rules. Following this preparatory work, the group decides what they would like to discuss next time (safeguarding issues) and where they would like to meet. The group is keen for Chen to continue in his role as facilitator. He is happy to do this too, but suggests a review and evaluation after the third meeting.

A model for effective group participation

A measure of the effectiveness of any social relationship is the amount of communication between the different people concerned. In an effective one to one relationship we would expect the two people to communicate roughly in equal measure, so fifty per cent each. In a group of three or more, each member will listen more than they speak if everyone is going to have an opportunity to share their thoughts and views. When thinking about effective communication in groups, the Listen Observe Speak (LOS) model is useful.

Listen

It is important that all group members listen attentively to what each person says. Effective listening underpins all effective human relationships and as human beings we all need to be listened to as this makes us feel valued as people. Active listening means listening with a purpose and showing that you are listening. It includes reflecting, paraphrasing, restating and summarising what people have said (Culley and Bond, 2011). All of these responses help people to know that they have been listened to and need to be done tentatively by using phrases like 'You seem to be saying . . .' and 'It seems to me that . . .'. This gives people the opportunity to disagree with your interpretation when appropriate, for example by saying 'Not really, what I meant was . . .'. In particular, summarising is a very useful skill in helping to keep a discussion flowing and 'on track'.

Observe

All groups demonstrate different group dynamics and as a group member or facilitator it is important to observe how people interact with one another. Observing and listening are done concurrently, and observing how people speak and act gives important clues regarding how they might feel and how important certain issues are to them. Observing body language is particularly important, as through this we can gauge how comfortable people are in the discussion and can identify times when they seem to 'shut down' by folding their arms, crossing their legs or gazing out of the window. Being careful to observe also means we are thinking before we speak rather than simply speaking straight away.

Speak

It goes without saying that in order to listen effectively others need to communicate with us. So the questions posed need to be open, in order to give people the room to speak freely. Open questions start with words like when, where and how. Starting a question with why needs to be done with caution to ensure that it is not accusatory. Here, the tone of voice is all important; in a harsh tone, 'Why?' can easily become 'Why (on earth)?' It will be important to avoid closed questions, for example those that start with 'Do you . . .' as these demand an answer of yes or no and give people little opportunity to speak. However, they can be useful if particular group members are dominating a discussion.

Hypothetical questions can be a very powerful mechanism to use in challenging and sensitive situations and can help you to avoid offering solutions. Hypothetical questions can serve to remove the personal nature of a question and can help people think things through from a range of different perspectives. For example, questions such as 'Let's imagine we are the client. How would we feel?' and 'If we came across this again, how would we like to react?' can help us to step back and analyse a situation at a deeper level.

In challenging everyday practice, it is important to remember that we all need an opportunity to 'offload', but as a group member it is important to make sure that our contributions are relevant to the discussion and that we do not drift off at a tangent. Watching ourselves is a skill that we can develop to ensure that we are not either dominating a conversation or offering too few contributions.

Reflective activity 9.3

When you are next part of the group, try to practise using the LOS model. What do you notice about how the group communicates?

Case study 9.3

A group of student nurses decide to meet together to support one another in their studies. They meet each week and find it helpful in the following ways. By listening, they hear the perspectives of other people and, because there are a variety of people in the group with different strengths, they find they can help and support one another in areas where they feel they are weaker. This is particularly helpful when sharing their lecture notes as, invariably, different group members have noted down different things. They enjoy observing the dynamics of the group and make sure that everyone has the opportunity to participate. They all speak freely and take a questioning approach to debate relevant issues. This helps them to develop their skills of critical thinking, and they make sure that no one dominates the discussions.

Dangers and downsides

In any group situation issues and difficulties can arise. Here are some common ones and some suggested strategies for dealing with them.

- One person always dominates discussions – ask for contributions from other people in the group, whilst being appreciative of what everyone says. A phrase like 'It would be good to hear what others think' can be useful. If the person still wants to say more, offer to have a discussion after the session so they feel that their views are valued.
- Certain individuals never seem to participate – divide the group into pairs and be sure to put the quieter people together. That way they will have to speak to one another and will also have to share with the whole group when you ask for feedback.
- One person seems to feel very uncomfortable – speak to them individually in a break or at the end of the session. Remember to be tentative by using phrases like 'You seem to

be uncomfortable today. Is there something you would like to talk about?' Again, if they say no, this must be respected.

- The whole group is very quiet and reserved – many quiet people find it easier to talk in a pair or three, so again splitting into smaller groups can be helpful.
- The whole group will not stop talking – asking the group to take some time to write some reflections on relevant chosen areas can calm things down. If this becomes a pattern during meetings, asking group members to write things down before the meeting and to bring notes with them can help to achieve a sharper focus.
- The group is distracted and wanders off into other topics – remind them of the original question or area for discussion to guide them back to their focus. At times you may simply have to 'call a halt' to very lengthy discussions and move on to the next topic.
- Someone makes an offensive comment (for example racist, sexist) – take a sensitively challenging approach and ask a question such as 'I'm wondering what made you say that. Can you please elaborate on that?' makes the person think far more than 'That's offensive . . .'
- You find that you dislike one group member – remember you are human and nobody likes everyone. The same applies to any group member that you feel does not like you.
- Sessions that last too long – be very clear beforehand how long a session is due to last and keep to it. If necessary, carry things over to the next meeting rather than allowing the session to continue indefinitely.

Sample exercises

This section contains some exercises that can be used in groups to help people reflect on their practice at a deeper level. Whilst discussion is good, a well planned exercise can enable a sharper focus and prompt deeper reflection.

- Prompt questions – a general question that helps people to reflect on their practice. For example, 'Since we last met, what have you been most proud of in your practice?' and 'Which particular situation has challenged you the most?'
- Quotes – find an appropriate quote and ask people to discuss it. There are many websites that offer a wide range of useful quotes, such as www.brainyquotes.com which organises quotes under themes.
- Presenting challenging cases – ask group members to write up a challenging case and bring it to the group for discussion.
- Give group members a short piece to read before the session and discuss it.
- Ask the group to identify a theme that they would like to focus on and ask one of the members to lead a discussion.
- Use role play to help people to develop their practice, for example by focusing on listening skills or assertiveness.
- Ask group members to watch a video (for example on YouTube) and to make notes. Then ask them to share their notes as a exercise in observation.
- Rosy glow exercise – give each participant a sheet of paper and ask them to write their name at the top of it. Sitting in a circle, pass all the sheets round clockwise person

by person. Ask people to write a positive comment expressing something that they appreciate in the person whose name is at the top of the sheet and then fold the paper over so that no one else can read it. Do this until each person has written on each of the sheets and the person gets their own sheet back. Encourage people to take the sheet and to read it when they get home. They might want to keep it in the top drawer of their desk or in their bag for the days when they feel like resigning!

- The talking stick – this is a very helpful technique to make sure that people are heard and understood. The talking stick (this can be any type of stick or even a pencil); only the person who holds the stick is allowed to speak. The people listening can pose sensitive questions for the purpose of clarification to make sure they have understood the points being made. When the person speaking feels they have said all they want to say and have been understood, they then pass the stick on to the person who wants to speak next.

Conclusion

In this chapter we have considered a wide range of issues in relation to reflecting in groups. It is clear that we can learn a lot by reflecting on our own and with a critical friend. Reflecting in a group can open up wider discussions and broaden our perspectives. Group facilitation is a very skillful activity and something that we can learn by observation and practice. In the next chapter we move on to consider the area of managing change.

References

Bager-Charleson, S. (2010) *Reflective Practice in Counselling and Psychotherapy*, Exeter: Learning Matters.
Cowie, H. and Wallace, P. (2000) *Peer Support in Action: From Bystanding to Standing by*, London: Sage.
Culley, S. and Bond, T. (2011) *Integrative Counselling Skills in Action*, 3rd edn. London: Sage.
Forsyth, D.R. (2006) *Group Dynamics*, 4th edn, Belmont, CA: Wadsworth Publishing.
Johns, C. (2013) *Becoming a Reflective Practitioner*, 4th edn. Chichester: Wiley-Blackwell.
Revans, R. (2011) *ABC of Action Learning*, Farnham, Surrey: Gower Publishing Ltd.
Thompson, N. (2011) *Effective Communication: A Guide for the People Professions*, Basingstoke: Palgrave Macmillan.
Wheatley, M.J. (2012) 'Is the pace of life hindering our ability to manage?' Available from www.margaret wheatley.com/articles/the pace of life.html. Accessed 7 May 2015.

10 Managing change

'The only thing that is constant is change.'

(Heraclitus)

Introduction

In this chapter we will explore the nature of change and how it can be managed. Some seminal theories of change will be examined, which can help us to devise effective strategies for managing change. It is worth noting that these models can also be used very effectively with clients as well as in our own reflective development. The chapter will conclude with a model for action.

Why having an understanding of change is important for professional practitioners

Change is a particularly relevant topic for many people who are working, not only those who are in roles where they are supporting people. Many practitioners say that they experience a lot of regular and ongoing change in their work. As a result, they have to learn how to manage change and continuously adapt their ways of working to suit new requirements. Many areas of professional practice are governed by policy, and a change of government can spark wide-ranging change in certain sectors (for example, in education). Having an understanding of change theories can help us to identify why we can experience certain things when we are faced with change. This understanding also helps us to see what might happen next and enables us to plan more effectively for what we could face in the future; many aspects of change are unpredictable, so the words 'might' and 'could' are particularly pertinent here.

Constant change and its effects

Many people agree that there are few things in life that stay the same. For many, the pace and amount of change that they experience in their lives is great and, at times, fast and furious; it can even be overwhelming. If you work, or hope to work in any professional area supporting people, you can expect your own practice to be subject to change on a regular basis. In addition, you may well find yourself working with clients who are experiencing significant change in their lives. Understanding the effects of change and the ways that change manifests itself in the people you are seeking to support is vital for effective professional practice.

Change is often difficult, because inevitably it involves loss. Most of us are 'creatures of habit' and feel safe and secure when we know what we are doing and thereby know what to expect. By contrast, when we experience change we can feel insecure and anxious. If we see a particular change as positive, we might overall find the process of change easier, but even then we can long for things to be familiar. Conversely, even when we perceive a situation as being very negative, we can still prefer the security of knowing the current situation to the uncertainty of not knowing what the future might bring. As a result, change and stress often go 'hand in hand'. The topic of stress is examined in some detail in the next chapter where the subject of 'mindfulness' is explored. However, we will inevitably touch on issues of stress in this chapter too as it is often (but not always) a manifestation of people's experiences of change.

It is important to understand what causes change in professional practice and here are some of the main reasons:

- People change – in all areas of professional practice, people change as they learn and develop. Good people have a habit of moving on (and sometimes up too), so if you currently work with an excellent practitioner or manager, you may find that before too long they move on. This is likely to be both disappointing and challenging at one and the same time.
- Circumstances change – a wide range of things can affect our circumstances and we may suddenly find that we have challenging things to deal with in our personal and professional lives. The Holmes and Rahe (1967) Social Readjustment Rating Scale ranks the changes in our lives that cause us most stress with bereavement and divorce being the highest on the scale and holidays and Christmas being surprisingly high!
- Work changes – over a number of years we have seen fundamental changes in the labour market that have had a marked effect on people's experiences of work. The impact of Information and Communication Technology (ICT) has been profound in many areas of working life, and many of us are expected to be 'self servicing' in areas like administration when this might not be our particular strength. ICT also means that work can no longer only be done in our place of work, and remote desktop working from home or from 'hot desks' has become commonplace for many professionals. Whilst this can have many positive aspects, it also means that the boundaries between work and home life have become blurred, which can lead to a struggle regarding work/life balance. In addition, the advent of compulsory competitive tendering in the public sector in the early 1980s meant that many services were outsourced. Jobs that had once been seen as secure became subject to things like short-term employment contracts, consultancy activity and regular contract renewals, the latter often involving individuals having to 'apply for their own jobs'.
- Professions change – particularly when professions are led, or at least heavily influenced by government policy, change can be rapid and extensive. For example, the latest statistics on achievement in schools can affect education policy as governments strive to be seen to do better than their predecessors. The latest child protection case to 'hit' the media can force governments and local authorities to act swiftly and decisively, putting practitioners under immense pressure to get things 'right'.

Having an understanding of theories of change can help us to gain insights into what we see, think and feel when we experience change.

Adams, Hayes and Hopson's model

There are a number of theories that seek to describe and explain the process of change and one of these is Adams, Hayes and Hopson's (1976) transition model. Adams et al. (1976: 7) define transition as a 'discontinuity in a person's life space', which can be either expected or unexpected. Their transition curve offers a clear explanation of what happens to people when they experience change and is used in a variety of settings, including bereavement counselling. The curve is depicted as a wave – viewed from left to right, it is drawn as a line that rises initially, falls steeply and then rises again on the right.

As we experience transition it is common to experience a range of different feelings as we progress through this process. In their seminal work, Adams, et al. (1976) describe the following seven stages or phases of the transition process:

Stage 1 – Immobilisation (the curve rises). As the process starts and we begin to get used to the idea of change, we can have feelings of being overwhelmed by the enormity of what is happening. This can mean that we 'freeze' and become unable to take any action. We might not know which way to turn as we try to take in the whole idea of change.

Stage 2 – Reaction. As we begin to realise that change is happening, we can react to it in two different ways. If we see the transition as being positive, we can feel elated and even excited. If we feel negative about the change we can have a sense of despair. Either way, we then begin a process of minimisation (a form of denial) where we consider that the change may not be as big an issue as we initially thought. For example, if we feel elated because we have been offered a job, we come back down to earth when we begin to see that we will now have to do the work. If we feel disappointed because we haven't been offered a job, we question how much we really wanted it anyway.

Stage 3 – Self-doubt (the curve starts to dip). As the transition becomes more real, our thoughts turn to self-doubt and as our feelings continue to dip, we start to ask ourselves questions such as 'Can I really do this?' and 'Do I really want this?' The challenges presented by the change and the implications of it become ever more apparent and we can experience feelings of anger or apathy.

Stage 4 – Acceptance and letting go (the base of the curve is reached). Much of the focus of the process so far has been on looking back. As we reach the base of the curve and begin to accept that the change is happening, our thoughts begin to turn to the future and we start to let go of the past. However, the future is still very uncertain and we can feel as if we are stepping into the unknown. This can sometimes feel like a steep climb out of the base of the curve.

Stage 5 – Testing (the curve begins to move upwards again). As we begin to get used to the new situation, we try out new ways of doing things. This is all part of a process of finding coping strategies for managing the new situation and we probably feel more energised.

Stage 6 – Search for meaning. This is a period when we spend some time reflecting on what has happened in order to explore what the change means for us. It also helps us to think about how we managed the transition, and from this we learn how we might manage the next one that comes along.

Stage 7 – Integration (the end of the curve is reached). In this stage the transition is internalised and change is accepted fully into our everyday lives.

Over the years this model has also been critiqued, raising questions such as whether the stages can be identified as specifically as claimed and whether individuals make specific plans for change as suggested. However, it is clear that this model shows us that we often go through highs and lows over a period of time as we experience change. It is important to understand that people will often experience the stages on the curve more than once, going backwards and forwards several times re-visiting certain stages. Some people will not complete the curve, but will remain in self-doubt at the base of the curve and fail to accept the change or let go of the past. Others will continue to test out new strategies or search for meaning and not everyone will reach the stage of integration. This particular model is very helpful in describing the transition process and can be used very effectively with clients to help them to understand this process too. Showing clients the transition curve and discussing their experiences of change in relation to it can help them to see where they are in relation to the stages and what they might expect in the future.

Reflective activity 10.1

Now think about a transition you have been through recently. Can you identify the stages of this model in relation to what you experienced? Now think about someone you are working with who is experiencing change. Can you identify aspects of their feelings and behaviours that show the different stages of the model?

Case study 10.1

Igor is a social worker who works with families who are hoping to adopt children. He can see the prospective parents he is working with going through the various stages of the transition curve and he finds it helpful to explain this to them so that they know what they might expect in the future. Igor himself is currently experiencing transition as his service is being re-organised in the light of recent announcements about public sector cuts. Igor feels that his future is uncertain, but is also keen to look at his options for the future. Over the next few weeks Igor makes some notes in his journal under the headings of the transition curve to try and clarify what is happening in his life.

Stage 1 – Immobilisation. I suppose I felt a bit numb when the cuts were announced today. My life is on hold again. Better not book that holiday after all.

Stage 2 – Reaction. Well, I got through it last time, so I guess I can do it again. It can't be that bad really.

(continued)

(continued)

Stage 3 – Self-doubt. So now they've announced how many posts there will be and it's scary. I haven't been here that long, so it's easy and cheap to get rid of me. I'm not sure I can cope with this again. How can they do this to us? It's so unfair. We do a good job and how can they expect us to do more than we are doing already? We have so many needy children who need good homes.

Stage 4 – Acceptance and letting go. So the posts have been advertised and I now need to apply. I've started looking for other jobs too – better to be safe than sorry. I do enjoy my work and I've decided I do want to continue if I can. It's all really quite scary.

Stage 5 – Testing. They've offered us some support with job applications and interviews, so I've booked myself onto a course. My friend who works in HR in another authority has also offered to help me. We are going to have a mock interview together. Hopefully things are looking up.

Stage 6 – Search for meaning. So I went for interview and have just heard that I was successful. Thank goodness I went for that help with my applications. Several people I know have not been appointed and some of them are good workers. They didn't seem to take the process very seriously though. This is a real lesson for when (and I mean when) this happens again.

Stage 7 – Integration. My new post starts in a few weeks time. I'll be in a different team with a new manager and it will take me a while to get used to it. But it feels like I'm coming out on the other side. Time to book that holiday!

Bridges

A simpler, but no less useful model of transition is a three-stage model put forward by Bridges (2004). Bridges argues that all transitions start with endings and end with beginnings, and in his model all three stages overlap. Stage one, 'endings', implies that we experience loss at the beginning of the process as we let go of what is behind us. This is followed by stage two, 'the neutral zone', which can be an uncomfortable place where we can feel anxious and uncertain about what lies ahead. Bridges argues that we need to spend time here so that we can discover what we should do next. Often we will feel as if we are in some kind of 'limbo'. The final stage is 'new beginnings' as we move forward into the next phase of our lives.

The work of Kurt Lewin

Taking an analytical approach to change can help us to understand more about it and how we might cope with it. As a result of his work on organisational development, Lewin developed two very useful theories that serve as analytical tools to help us to understand how change can be managed.

The first of these is Lewin's (1951) field theory, often referred to as force field analysis where he used a scientific approach and applied it to social situations (see Figure 10.1). In all

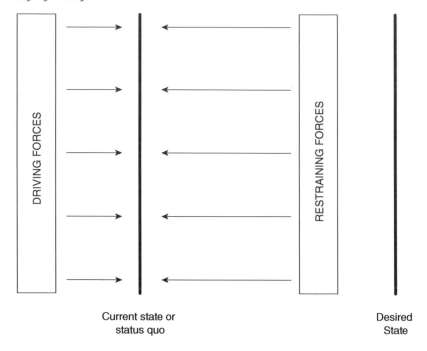

Current state or
status quo

Desired
State

Figure 10.1 Lewin's field theory

situations he identified that there are forces at work that promote change (he called these driving forces) and those that resist it and even work against it (restraining forces). Each of these two forces pulls against the other in opposite directions. A situation or circumstance is then held in balance in the present (the status quo) by the tension caused by the interaction between the two forces. Lewin calls this balance 'quasi stationary equilibrium', which is constantly in a state of flux.

Movement towards what Lewin calls the 'desired state' involves change and this can happen in one of two ways. Either the driving forces need to be maximised or the restraining forces need to be minimised to prompt change. When both happen together the amount of change achieved is greatest.

Reflective activity 10.2

Now think of a situation you have experienced recently where you have needed to make a change in your professional practice. Using Lewin's field theory, what were the driving forces and where were the restraining forces? Which were strongest and what was the result?

Viewed alongside these ideas of a force field, Lewin (1951) also developed his three-step model to describe organisational and other types of change. The three steps are as follows:

Step 1 – Unfreezing, here the 'quasi stationary equilibrium' needs to be de-stabilised before old behaviours can be discarded. This is a difficult process and can involve us becoming aware of such things as complacency and habit. Lewin saw change as a profound psychological and dynamic process and in this first step we can expect the restraining forces to be at work as they try to prevent us from engaging with change.

Step 2 – Moving, or encouraging the development of new ideas. This is often achieved through an iterative process of action research where current scenarios are analysed in order to identify how change can be promoted and best achieved. Focusing on maximising the driving forces and minimising the restraining forces is important at this point in order to achieve change.

Step 3 – Re-freezing, this involves stabilising the changes into the new state of 'quasi stationary equilibrium'. Lewin recognised that change could be short-lived if it was not reinforced, and unless this happens it is easy to slip back into old practices.

Reflective activity 10.3

Consider again the situation you identified in Reflective Activity 2 and examine it in relation to Lewin's three-step model. Can you identify the three steps?

Case study 10.2

Steven is a primary school teacher who has been working for the past three years with children in Year 1. He enjoys his work very much and feels settled in his current role. Steven knows that the Head Teacher has a policy of moving staff round the different year groups to enhance their professional development. He also knows that several teachers are leaving this year and that the school will be short of teachers in Year 6. When the Head asks Steven to teach a Year 6 class next year he feels very unhappy and annoyed. He makes it clear that he would like to stay where he is, but the Head says that this needs to happen and assures him that it will be good for his overall career development. Steven is still unhappy when he says goodbye to the children on the final day of term, and over the summer he begins to dread the start of the next term. Going back to school is difficult, but Steven finds that working in a team with teachers in Key Stage 2 is different, particularly as each of them has a specialism. This gives Steven more time to spend teaching PE, which he enjoys. By Christmas Steven is feeling more settled and is enjoying interacting with older children and having conversations with them about transferring to secondary school.

Lewin's models remain very helpful tools for analysing our own responses to change, but also those of colleagues and clients. Lewin's theories, particularly his three-step model, have been critiqued in relation to their currency – whether they can be applied in their entirety today is questionable. For example, the concept of re-freezing could suggest the kind of stability that our fast paced and ever changing world never seems to have and is unlikely to have in the future. However, many argue that Lewin's theories have become seminal in the field of organisational behaviour and that aspects of them remain useful in today's world. Lewin's concept of the 'felt need for change' is also worthy of consideration and is closely linked with the next theory of change that we will now move on to examine.

Readiness for change

Being ready for change has a big impact on whether or not we engage with it as a process. Lewin identified that when there is a 'felt need for change', change is much more likely to happen. In many respects this is what makes enforced change particularly difficult to deal with, as when this happens we simply might not be ready for it.

In the same vein, Prochaska and DiClemente's (1983) work on change also identifies a number of stages in the change process, and includes stages when change is unlikely to happen; these are particularly worth noting. Their work has become prominent in relation to health and well being (for example in the area of addiction) and is frequently referred to as a transtheoretical model because it draws on a number of different theories of psychotherapy. The model has the following stages:

1   Pre-contemplation – here, the individual is not considering change in the near future and may be unaware of the need for it. They might be happy with their current situation or unhappy with it. Either way, they are not prepared or ready for change at the moment. In this stage the advantages of change are often minimised as the individual focuses their attention on all the disadvantages, thereby making change seem just too difficult to even think about. Often, this stage is characterised by the well-known phrase 'ignorance is bliss'.

2   Contemplation – now the individual is beginning to get ready for change. The balance between the pros and cons for change has become much more even, causing a degree of ambivalence as they try to make a decision for or against change. This ambivalence can cause procrastination, and here the individual can put off making a start in the change process.

3   Preparation – here, the person is ready for change and will start to take action soon. They begin by taking some small helpful steps forward like telling family and friends of their intentions but they also commonly experience a fear of possible failure.

4   Action – the individual is now fully engaged in the process of change and is working hard to continue their new behaviours. They are learning how to strengthen their commitment to change and identifying ways of resisting the urge to fall back into old habits.

5   Maintenance – the change in behaviour is now becoming embedded, but the person is still learning about those situations that can tempt them back into their old habits.

6   Termination – the change process is now complete. The individual is secure in their acceptance of change and their new behaviour has become somewhat automatic. They feel sure that they will not return to their old ways of doing things.

Whilst presented as a sequence, individuals are often seen travelling back and forth through the stages above. Often, this is as a result of 'slipping back' into old habits or ways of doing things. It is also clear that not everyone reaches the Termination stage, but can experience a sixth stage called Relapse as they resume their former ways.

Reflective activity 10.4

Now think of an example from your practice where Prochaska and DiClemente's model might offer a good description of your experiences. Describe it and identify each of the stages. Did you reach Termination? If so, what helped you? If not, what got in the way?

Case Study 10.3

Stephanie is starting the final year of her nursing degree and doesn't want it to end. She has made so many good friends and feels that she will lose touch with many of them as they all go their separate ways. As her friends start to apply for jobs, Stephanie feels ambivalent about looking for a job and prefers to wait until later in the year. But as the year progresses, people start to receive job offers and Stephanie begins to feel a bit left behind. She starts to look for vacancies on relevant websites but feels anxious about what the future holds. Following a few applications and three interviews, she is offered a job in a hospital; she is pleased about this as she knows one of her friends will be working there too. She hopes they might be able to share a flat together and begins to look forward to feeling settled in her new surroundings.

Having examined some theoretical models of change, it is clear that they each have similarities but also that they have their differences. Table 10.1 compares the models of Adams et al., Lewin and Prochaska and DiClemente to highlight these.

Table 10.1 Theoretical models of change

Adams, Hayes and Hopson	*Lewin's field theory and three-step model*	*Prochaska and DiClemente*
	No 'felt need' for change. The restraining forces are dominant	1. Pre-contemplation
1. Immobilisation		
	1. Unfreezing – balance between the driving and restraining forces becomes more equal	2. Contemplation
2. Reaction	1. Unfreezing – balance between the driving and restraining forces continues to become more equal	

(continued)

Table 10.1 (continued)

Adams, Hayes and Hopson	Lewin's field theory and three-step model	Prochaska and DiClemente
3. Self-doubt	1. Unfreezing – the restraining forces come back to the foreground	
	1. Unfreezing – the driving forces become more dominant	3. Preparation
4. Acceptance and letting go	2. Moving – the driving forces are maximised and the restraining forces are minimised	4. Action
5. Testing	2. Moving – continuing awareness of the need to keep the restraining forces 'at bay'	5. Maintenance
6. Search for meaning		
7. Integration	3. Re-freezing – 'quasi stationary equilibrium' is reached	6. Termination
		Relapse

Strategies for managing change

If change is inevitable, it is very important to have a number of strategies for managing it as effectively as possible. This is not meant to imply that change is something that we can all approach purely clinically or logically; very often our emotions will be involved in the process and a rational approach will only be helpful to a certain extent. Recognising change as it is happening can help us to cope with it better and, in addition, we can take some practical steps that might help too. Here are some suggestions:

- Remember that change always involves loss, so do not be surprised by a sense of sadness, even when you see the particular change as a positive one.
- Try to find out as much information as possible about the change in question. The famous phrase 'forewarned is forearmed' reminds us that knowledge is useful and can reduce our anxiety levels.
- If possible, find out the reasons for change. Understanding why things are happening can help us to cope with them better.
- Seek out support from other people, for example colleagues, friends and family.
- Where possible, try to become involved in the process of change. Having change 'done to you' can make you feel vulnerable and as if things are out of control. Taking an active part can help you to feel more in control.

Tschudi's (1977) ABC model can be a very effective tool for helping us to be clear about how we feel about change and the meaning we apply to it. It involves drawing a table with two

Table 10.2 Tschudi's ABC model

A1 Current scenario – my current job or role	A2 Future or desired scenario – my job in a re-structured or new organisation
B1 Disadvantages of the current scenario • I've been here a while, is it time to move on? • I feel I've learned all I can here • My role model and other colleagues have left • My work isn't challenging me any more • Will there be any opportunities for promotion?	B2 Advantages of the future or desired scenario • A new challenge • Chance to meet new people • Possibly a higher salary • New training and development opportunities • Lots to learn
C1 Advantages of the current scenario • Feeling secure • Feeling confident in my ability to do a good job • Recognised for what I do • 'Knowing the ropes'	C2 Disadvantages of the future or desired scenario • Feeling insecure • Lacking confidence in a new situation • Needing to learn things 'from scratch' again • Being the new person again

columns; on the left hand side is the current scenario and on the right the preferred or future scenario. The table then asks us to identify the respective advantages and disadvantages of the proposed change. Table 10.2 illustrates how it can be used and the change in question is a change of job or work role.

Reflective activity 10.5

Now use the ABC model to analyse a change that you have experienced. Make notes in each of the columns. What does this show you about how you manage change?

Back to assumptions

In Chapter 7 we examined the whole area of assumptions and, when considering change, this too is something that we can often make assumptions about. In the field of education and from a management perspective, Fullan's (2001) work on managing change has been particularly influential and his ten assumptions about change are worthy of note. They are as follows:

1 Do not assume that your version of what the change should be is what could or should happen.
2 Assume that change involves a certain amount of ambiguity and uncertainty; this can be, and often is, unsettling. People need to work out their own meaning, which will come about in a process of clarification through reflective practice.
3 Assume that conflict and disagreement are inevitable and, indeed, fundamental. If these are not evident, it is likely that little is changing.

4   Assume that people need pressure to change; most people are happier with the status quo simply because it is familiar.
5   Assume that effective change takes time. Successful change requires a high level of commitment.
6   Do not assume that a lack of change implementation means that the change itself has been rejected. There may be other reasons like inadequate resources or that insufficient time has elapsed for the change to become embedded into practice.
7   Do not assume that everyone will change or expect them to do so.
8   Assume that you will need a good plan for change to happen effectively.
9   Assume that you will never know everything, or even enough, to make a decision regarding what action you should take.
10 Assume that changing the culture of an organisation is at the heart of the change process, not just implementing particular innovations.

Reflective activity 10.6

Which of Fullan's ten assumptions do you find the most applicable to your situation and why?

Conclusion

In this chapter we have explored the area of managing change. Having examined a number of theoretical approaches can help us to recognise various aspects of change and to understand more about our responses to it. In the next chapter we will move on to explore reflective practice as a way of being, including the area of mindfulness in professional practice.

References

Adams, J., Hayes, J. and Hopson, B. (1976) *Transition: Understanding and Managing Personal Change*, London: Martin Robertson.
Bridges, W. (2004) *Transitions: Making Sense of Life's Changes*, Cambridge, MA: Da Capo Press.
Fullan, M. (2001) *The New Meaning of Educational Change*, 3rd edn, London: RoutledgeFalmer.
Holmes, T.H. and Rahe, R.H. (1967) 'The social readjustment rating scale', *Journal of Psychosomatic Research*, 11(2): 213-18.
Lewin, K. (1951) *Field Theory in Social Science: Selected Theoretical Papers*, New York: Harper and Row.
Prochaska, J.O. and DiClemente, C.C. (1983) 'Stages and processes of self-change of smoking: toward an integrative model of change', *Journal of Consulting and Clinical Psychology*, 51(3): 390-5.
Tschudi, F. (1977) 'Loaded and honest questions: a construct theory view of symptoms and therapy', in D. Bannister (ed.) *New Perspectives in Personal Construct Theory*, London: Academic Press.

11 Critically reflective practice as a way of being

> 'Follow effective action with quiet reflection. From the quiet reflection will come even more effective action.'
>
> (Peter Drucker, 2011)

Introduction

At this point in our journey it is time to revisit the overall purpose of the book and its structure. We began by examining some of the fundamental tenets of reflective practice and learning from experience. As we have progressed towards an understanding of critically reflective practice, we have explored issues of coping with our emotional responses and challenging our assumptions. We have also considered the role of feedback in professional development and how we can reflect in groups. The previous chapter looked at the management of change and now we are moving on as we seek to embed critically reflective practice into our everyday work and lives.

This chapter will begin with a review of the term critically reflective practice and will include a discussion of the term reflexivity. We will then explore some key elements of the work of Johns and return to some of Brookfield's work, both of which help us to examine how we can reflect at a deeper level in an ongoing way. The chapter will conclude with an exploration of the area of managing stress, mindfulness and Covey's useful concept of 'sharpening the saw'.

Critically reflective practice and reflexivity

The concept of reflective practice has been subject to criticism in a number of ways. Some suggest that it is obvious that we need to think about our practice and so discount the notion of doing this in a deliberate way, whilst others point to the difficulties that practitioners experience in trying to take a reflective approach in their busy professional lives (Finlay, 2008). It is also easy to see that the term can be used by different people to mean different things to suit their own circumstances. Writing from the context of teacher education, Loughran (2002) suggests adding the word effective before the term reflective practice.

More recently some writers have added the word critically before the term reflective practice (Thompson and Thompson, 2008). This suggests that it is not enough simply to reflect on our experience, but that we need to take a critical approach too. It is important to remember that this does not mean that we only focus on negative aspects of our practice, but see the positives too. In this way we formulate a critique of our practice (like the food critic in Chapter 3) and do not fall into the trap of becoming weighed down by negative criticism and any kind of idea that we are never good enough.

Critically reflective practice is underpinned by reflexivity, as the term reflexivity has the potential to be confusing. Initial thoughts might lead us to assume that reflexivity is about our reflex actions or those things that we do automatically; however, the opposite is in fact the case. Until fairly recently the term reflexivity was used in the context of research – meaning the ability to see the things that are influencing our thoughts, behaviours and actions (Fook and Askeland, 2006). This is particularly important in research because, without reflexivity, we can fall into the trap of simply seeing what we expect to see, and our conclusions then become predictable. In professional practice reflexivity means that we are aware of how we think, feel and act and the assumptions we might be making. In addition, reflexivity also makes us aware of issues of power in relationships and organisations. Hence, the chapters in this book have been presented in a particular order to take us on a journey from reflection on experience, processing our feelings and questioning our assumptions in order to prompt critical reflection and reflexivity. It is also important to remember that as our focus broadens from simply being aware of ourselves (see Chapter 2) to being aware of our social and political context, we become mindful of issues of power evident in all social relationships. It is only when we recognise and understand these issues that we can seek to work in an anti discriminatory way.

Reflexivity is not only being mindful of ourselves and the part we play in the process; Fook and Askeland (2006) remind us that it also involves being clear about our context and the impact this can have on our practice. In all professional relationships it is important to have an understanding of issues of power and how these are played out in our working environments. In relation to working with clients, we need to remember that issues of power will always be present and that clients usually feel that the power lies with the professional practitioner and not with them. Indeed, in some areas of professional practice (such as teaching and social work) it seems clear that this is the case. For example, in classrooms, teachers need to maintain a positive learning environment for all students, which can involve applying sanctions for those who are reluctant to engage in the learning process. Social workers can be seen to hold the power when it comes to such issues as child protection and work with vulnerable adults. However, whilst recognising this, we also need to question our overall aims and what we are ultimately trying to achieve. For example, if young people in schools are going to progress to higher education, allowing them greater independence in the later years of schooling will prepare them well for their future studies. The social work profession recognises the need to be very cognisant of issues of power and its potential misuse, which can lead to discriminatory and even oppressive practice (Thompson, 2012). Issues of power can particularly be seen at work within certain professions. For example, Johns (2013) argues strongly that as part of a profession dominated by women, many nurses experience patriarchal attitudes and practices that can oppress them. In all of these cases an argument can be made for the handing over of at least some of the power that practitioners hold.

Reflective activity 11.1

Now think about your own workplace and consider the issues of power that are evident. How might you want to try and influence some of these for change? What difficulties might you expect in trying to do this?

Case study 11.1

Adam is head of the sixth form in a large comprehensive school. Many of the students go on to study at a range of different universities, locally and nationally and Adam feels it is important that they are well prepared for their further studies. Adam remembers struggling when he went to university as he no longer had the support from his school teachers that he had come to rely on. He is keen for the students to become more independent in their learning and development so that they can thrive in the sixth form and in their further studies. Adam decides to work with his team of tutors to design a programme of sessions to help the students to manage themselves better, which should be beneficial for them now and in the future. The programme includes sessions in tutorial time on a range of relevant topics including time management and meeting deadlines; a range of study skills such as effective reading, note taking and referencing in academic work; managing stress and coping with change. In order to achieve the overall goal of students becoming more independent learners, the students are asked to work together in small groups to prepare one of the sessions, to give a presentation and to lead a discussion on it. They are also asked to put together materials for all students to use on the school's virtual learning environment. Each group works with a tutor who acts as a facilitator; the tutors are asked to allow the students to work in ways that suit them, handing over the responsibility for the sessions to them. They are also asked to give feedback to the students on how they are working together and the quality of the work they are producing both during their preparation time and after they have delivered their session.

Being open to change

In Chapter 2 we discussed the notion that when looking at our practice in a metaphorical mirror we might discover things that need to change. Whether or not we then take action to make that change is a choice. However, maintaining a position where we are open to change is vital in professional practice. Fay (1987) discusses three important aspects of critical reflection: curiosity, commitment and intelligence, which are considered by Johns (2013) and are relevant to the whole area of critical reflection and change. Maintaining curiosity in professional practice is vital if our work is to continue to stimulate and challenge us. Posing questions such as 'What is happening here?', 'What made the person respond in that way?' and 'Was I as helpful to that person as I might have been?' help to make our practice sharp and keep us open to new possibilities. Losing our curiosity means that we lose our creativity and run the risk of our practice becoming mundane and even defensive.

Commitment helps us to maintain our energy for our practice and reminds us of why we do the work we are engaged in. This is particularly important at those times when, for good reasons, we can question why we continue working in our particular sector. Whether this is because of increasing workloads caused by budget cuts, managers that do not appear to be on our 'wave length', or simply a number of very challenging clients we are working with at the time, we can, and realistically should, expect our commitment to be challenged. This means that we need to remind ourselves of our reasons for doing the work we do and re-evaluating our position in order to incorporate any changes we might need to make.

Intelligent practitioners are insightful and view every situation as an opportunity for learning. They are slow to jump to conclusions and to dismiss things without paying them adequate attention. In short, they are continuously open to new ideas and will judge things on their merits rather than accepting or dismissing things at face value.

Another word that Johns considers at various points in his work is that of compassion. Many practitioners enter the helping professions because they want to support people and feel that they are making a difference. They have a sense of compassion, which enhances their curiosity and commitment and makes them intelligent practitioners. In addition, it gives them a passion for their work. In my own field of career development I continue to be excited by the potential of people to fulfil and sometimes exceed their own and society's expectations of them. Without compassion this becomes difficult. However, compassion is not a 'touchy feely' term that only involves feeling sympathy, but rather a driving force for social justice and emancipation.

Being open to change is not as easy as it might first appear and it is important that we are not naïve. Johns (2013: 6) warns us of the power of embodiment, which he describes as 'the way people normally think, feel and respond to the world in a normative and largely pre-reflective way'. In other words, in our places of work we may well see practices that serve to accept the way things are done currently and maintain the status quo, rather than opening up possibilities for change. This can even be the case when things are not working well; this might be because policy or legislation restricts what we can do, or sometimes it is simply because it is the easiest option. In such situations change on the part of the individual practitioner in their own work can be difficult to achieve.

The work of Johns

As a writer and researcher, Johns is a good example of someone who has continually been open to change and who, as a result, has developed his thinking over a number of years. In his recent work (Johns, 2013), some key concepts stand out in relation to critical reflection and reflexivity that are worthy of consideration here.

Enlightenment, empowerment and emancipation

Johns sees reflection as an action-oriented, day-to-day reality and certainly far removed from any kind of 'navel gazing'. In addition, reflection cannot be neutral but is 'a political and cultural movement towards creating a better, more caring and humane world' (Johns, 2013: 6). Such strong words remind us of the importance of compassion and are far removed from a simple (or even simplistic) approach that sees reflection as single loop learning (Kolb, 1984). Reflection is seen as part of a continuous process of enlightenment where we examine ourselves and our context and seek to understand why things are as they are and why things happen as they do. Empowerment means that we then look for ways of taking action on our new understandings, and emancipation happens as situations are transformed for a vision to be realised. It goes without saying that none of this is easy to achieve and such change can take time and a lot of effort. However, it is important not to lose sight of our vision for our practice if we are to maintain our levels of motivation and commitment (see Chapter 12 and the work of Senge).

Aesthetics, artistry and practical wisdom

Aesthetics is a branch of philosophy related to the study of art and, in particular, beauty. It is a word that is not often associated with professional practice and Johns also includes performance in his definition as he imagines a nurse going about her regular duties. Johns (2013: 45) describes the following four movements as 'the aesthetic response' for effective action. All four movements involve looking back on a situation and here they are expressed as questions.

1   How did I appreciate/assess the situation and identify the focus for my intervention?
2   How did I make the decisions to meet the desired outcomes?
3   How did I respond with appropriate and skilled action to meet the outcomes and to remain in tune with my values?
4   Were the outcomes met and were these also in tune with my values?

The idea of artistry in professional practice is a reminder of its unique nature involving a high level of skill. Any painter who is asked to reproduce a copy of a particular piece of work knows that it is highly unlikely that it will turn out to be exactly the same as the original. The original piece of art was created in particular circumstances and influenced by such things as light, dark and shade and the mood of the artist at the time. In the same way, highly skilled professional practice cannot be reproduced at will, although undoubtedly many students in training might wish that it could be!

Wisdom is a word most often associated with a person who has lots of knowledge and experience. Johns uses the term 'practical wisdom' to describe a practitioner's ability to assess a situation and to gauge the likely outcomes based on previous experience. This practical wisdom can be seen in practitioners who have grasped their personal understandings (or praxis) of their work through reflection. Such practitioners see their practice as fluid and constantly changing, as each situation and client they face is unique.

Typology of reflective practice

Johns' typology of reflective practice offers a useful summary of different aspects of reflection. It is broken down into the following five steps, which move from doing reflection to being reflective:

1   Reflection-on-experience – here, the practitioner reflects on a particular experience after it happens so that it can inform their future practice. This has resonance with Kolb's (1984) cycle.
2   Reflection-in-action – here, the practitioner stands back and seeks to see the situation differently in order to make progress towards a more desired outcome. This resonates with Schön's (1983) term, but helpfully includes the use of the term 'reframing'.
3   The internal supervisor – this is a dialogue that the practitioner has with themselves whilst having a conversation with another person as part of a process of making sense of the situation.
4   Reflection-within-the-moment – here, the practitioner is mindful of their patterns of thoughts, feelings and actions and is maintaining a focus on desirable practice.
5   Mindfulness – Johns describes this as seeing things as they really are without any distortion.

It is clear that people who are in training or new to professional practice can usefully start with reflection-on-experience as considered in the early chapters of this book. Mindfulness as described by Johns involves being aware moment by moment, and whether or not it is achievable seems questionable. However, as a goal it is certainly something that we should continue to strive for in professional practice.

Reflective activity 11.2

Consider some of the experienced practitioners you have worked with. Which of John's concepts do you see in evidence? In what ways?

Case study 11.2

Ola is an experienced nurse who works in a hospice. She faces many challenges in her work and regularly spends time reflecting on her practice. Ola is known as an excellent practitioner who is compassionate towards her patients. She sees patients as individuals and always seeks to make them as comfortable and relaxed as possible. She also offers vital support to relatives and friends, making them feel welcome, but always keeping an eye on how the patient is feeling as they are her major concern. Ola regularly spends time reflecting on what she has done each day; she does this on her own and in discussions with her critical friend. In many situations she thinks about things from different perspectives (particularly those of the patient) in order to continually work towards becoming the kind of nurse she wants to be. She often finds that she has

(continued)

(continued)

conversations with herself in her head whilst working with patients and this helps her to clarify what she is doing and why, and her previous experiences inform her actions. Ola loves her work because of the challenges it involves. She is always mindful of the patients' condition and this means that she can be calm and compassionate, whilst being realistic. This helps her to see the limitations of what she can do and 'keeps her feet on the ground'. She feels this prevents her from becoming overly emotionally involved with every patient she cares for and is then ready for the next challenge in her work.

Brookfield's lenses

Brookfield's (1995) work has become widely recognised for its insights into critically reflective practice. In his book *Becoming a Critically Reflective Teacher* he argues that there are four lenses through which we can reflect on practice critically. They are as follows:

1   Our own autobiographies as learners (and teachers for those who are training to teach) – this starts with an examination of our own stories and experiences of learning from the past, which enables us to begin to examine some of our deeply held values and assumptions about our practice and to begin to question them.
2   The eyes of our clients – viewing our practice from the point of view of our clients makes us more aware of issues of power in professional relationships.
3   The experiences of our colleagues – engaging in feedback processes can help us to see things we were not previously aware of, or those things in our Blind area (see the Johari Window in Chapter 8).
4   Theoretical literature – this can offer multiple explanations of phenomena, which can help us to understand that sometimes we are not responsible for things that happen in our practice.

Two particular lenses offer perspectives that we have not yet considered. The first lens of our own autobiography reminds us that we all have previous experiences of education and of life more broadly; these affect how we view the world and give us insights into the actions we might take or fail to take in the future. Narrative approaches argue that life is lived in story form; when we go home and talk about the day we have had, we tell a story rather than simply listing the things we have done. Narrative approaches have become influential in a wide range of professional areas, particularly in counselling, and here the argument is that looking back and telling our story then helps us to look forward and make decisions about how we want to act in the future. The fourth lens of theoretical literature reminds us that we can learn a lot from those who have written about professional practice, but also from those who have written from a theoretical point of view as well.

Brookfield argues for a deep level of critical reflection in the training of teachers and it is clear that in order to engage with this process we need to be ready to unearth things about ourselves that we may not find palatable; this can make us feel vulnerable. For example,

Klobassa (2014: 328) recommends using Brookfield's Critical Incident Questionnaire to break down barriers to discussions on issues of racism in order to 'encourage the trust and vulnerability necessary to interrogating race in significant and meaningful ways'. In order to make progress in our thinking about challenging issues, we need to make ourselves vulnerable. This needs to be done in a sensitive way, often by posing questions that help us to interrogate our practice fully. Brookfield argues that if we are teachers we need to do this with our students too.

Reflective activity 11.3

Now think of times when you have engaged in critical reflection using each of Brookfield's four lenses. Which of the four do you find the most helpful? Are there any that you are reluctant to use? Why might this be the case?

Case study 11.3

Rudolph is training to be a Careers Adviser. As part of one of his early sessions on his course he is asked to examine his own motivation for joining the profession. The tutor asks the students to write their story of how they came onto the course and Rudolph writes this.

At school I was always told I was bright, but I went to a really bad school where no one did any work. It's closed down now thank goodness. I managed to leave at sixteen with a few qualifications and went to a local FE college. It was like a second chance for me and I loved it. A lot of the students were adults who really wanted to work. Lots of them had had a bad time at school too and had got stuck in dead end jobs. They had come to college to try and turn their lives around. The atmosphere at college was completely different. I knew I wanted to go to university if I could, and soon met the college's Careers Advisers. They had a nice little office where you could go and chat at any time. They also handled all the UCAS forms and gave you lots of support in trying to decide what you wanted to study and with your personal statement. I remember saying to one of them one day that I would really like to do their job and the Careers Adviser gave me a lot of encouragement. I went on and did a degree and then applied for this postgraduate course. So here I am again – like when I was at the FE college, I am younger than most of the other students here, but this is good for me. I know I want to work with young people in schools, particularly those who might not be doing so well. I want to help them to achieve their potential and to give them the kind of support I received when I was trying to decide what I wanted to do in the future. It's great to know that I will be giving something back and I know from my experience that even if you feel you have had a bad start, you can go on to better things.

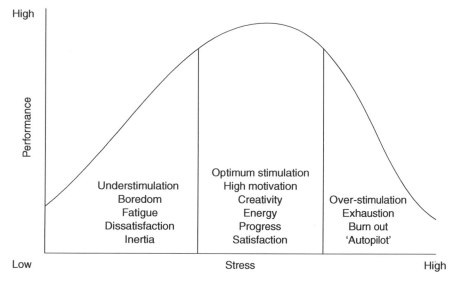

Figure 11.1 The stress curve

Managing stress

We all need a certain amount of stress in our lives in order to be able to perform at our best. However, too much stress leads to a high level of anxiety and, in extreme circumstances, to burn out. By contrast, too little stress can lead to boredom and lethargy. For example, going into an examination feeling totally at ease might mean that we lower our levels of concentration and fail to perform as well as we should. But being overly anxious in such a situation means that we might forget the things we know and again fail to do ourselves justice. Figure 11.1 illustrates the link between stress and performance.

In order to maintain effective performance, we need to remain in the centre of the curve as much as possible, and to do this we need to understand what causes us to experience stress. This will be different for different people, but some of the most common causes of stress are as follows:

- The environment – workplaces can be stressful places due to the demands they make on staff: for example, long and sometimes unsociable working hours, unclear role specifications, poor communication, inadequate leadership and management and lack of support.
- The individual – I can put pressure on myself: for example having unrealistically high expectations of what I can achieve and 'beating myself up' when I fail to achieve all I want to, feeling powerless to influence my working context, being passive and unable to say 'no' to the demands of others.
- The group – it is good to work with colleagues, but just as teenagers can often experience peer pressure, so in the same way peer pressure at work also exists: for example, feeling the need to agree to things in meetings when you want to disagree, being seen to achieve objectives and targets at the expense of your values, not taking all your annual leave because those around you do not take theirs.

Fontana (1989) highlights the following three groups of symptoms of stress:

1   Cognitive – stress affects our thought processes and too much stress can mean that we find it difficult to concentrate and are easily distracted. Our speed of response becomes slower and we make more mistakes. We fail to organise properly as we cannot assess accurately how long it will take us to do particular tasks and we can become confused and irrational.

2   Emotional – too much stress means that we cannot relax or 'switch off' and we worry about things a lot of the time and generally feel anxious. We can imagine that we are ill and our feelings of healthiness and well being disappear. We might change as people; for example a tidy person might become messy and a caring person could become cold and indifferent. Things that we usually feel anxious about become exaggerated and lead us to become over sensitive or defensive; this might lead to emotional outbursts. In extreme cases this can lead to depression as our self-esteem plummets.

3   Behavioural – our interests diminish, we lack enthusiasm, become cynical, our energy levels are low and our regular sleep patterns are interrupted. Absenteeism from work increases, new information is ignored even when it is helpful and we shift responsibilities on to others. We solve problems at an increasingly superficial level and can become unpredictable. Drug, caffeine and alcohol consumption can rise and, in extreme cases, suicide threats can be made.

Recognising the symptoms of stress is vital if we are then going to seek to manage it. It is equally important to recognise the signs of stress in our colleagues and our clients so that we can support them effectively. Managing our own stress levels can be done in a number of ways. However, it is important to emphasise that there is only ever so much we can do to manage stress and it is unlikely that we will be able to avoid it completely. The following strategies can help us to manage stress and perform effectively in an ongoing way. Remember that different things help different people and in all cases find what helps you and take some appropriate action.

- Time management – this can certainly go some way towards alleviating stress. If you ever feel that your work life is somewhat chaotic, Allen's (2002) book *Getting Things Done* offers a comprehensive time and self-organisation system. But remember it is like 'fishing by hand' and could work for a while, at which point you might then need to look for an alternative. Don't 'beat yourself up' if, or when, it stops working; look for something else.

- Assertiveness – many of us experience high levels of stress because we are passive, have strong Please People drivers (see Chapter 2) and cannot say 'no'. Lindenfield (2001: 3) describes assertiveness as 'behaviour which helps us to communicate our needs, wants and feelings to other people without in any way abusing their human rights'. She gives some very helpful strategies to enable us to avoid being passive and to be more assertive without being either aggressive or manipulative.

- Physical exercise – this uses up excess adrenalin, releases endorphins (our 'feel good' hormones), forces us to take some time out and provides a distraction from whatever is making us anxious.

- Relaxation techniques – most of these involve breathing exercises and relaxing each part of your body whilst lying down (see the next section on mindfulness). It is commonly understood that 20 minutes of relaxation is equal to two hours of sleep; hence this is a good option if you are finding it difficult to sleep.
- Build your support mechanisms – make sure that there are people around you who can support you. Remember that when they are feeling stressed you can, and should, reciprocate.
- Have some 'me' time – especially for those in the helping professions, who spend most of their time supporting other people. Try to take some time out on a regular basis to spend do things you enjoy.
- Set yourself some new challenges – it can help to maintain your levels of motivation if you aim to achieve certain things within a timeframe; this does not have to be related to work and, indeed, is probably better if it is not. If you enjoy music, it could be listening to a new album every week, learning to play the instrument that you have always wanted to, or reading books or magazines for pleasure.
- Avoid unhealthy habits – most of us seek comfort in challenging times, but can slip into unhealthy habits such as smoking, snacking and drinking (including caffeine). This means that we can experience a 'sugar rush' followed by a dip in our levels of energy.
- Retain a positive outlook – remember those times when you have been successful, appreciate the supportive people around you and change your perspective.
- Understand what you can and cannot change – Niebuhr's famous Serenity Prayer states 'God, grant me the serenity to accept the things I cannot change, The courage to change the things I can, And the wisdom to know the difference'. It is worth remembering that time and energy spent trying to change things that cannot be changed is wasted and wearing.

Reflective activity 11.4

Now think about your own levels of stress. What strategies could you use to ensure that you remain in the centre of the stress curve?

Case study 11.4

Louise is a social worker in a leaving care team who is finding her work increasingly stressful. She decides to discuss her situation in her next supervision session where she explains some of the things she is experiencing. Louise explains that she feels very tired a lot of the time. She often stays late at work and finds it very difficult to switch off when she gets home. She finds herself constantly thinking about all the things she needs to do and then cannot get to sleep. This makes her feel more tired; when she does finally get to sleep, she then wakes up early, often with a headache. During her discussion with her supervisor she is able to identify some strategies that she feels might help her. Louise feels that work is starting to take over her life and she decides

(continued)

(continued)

to try and re-establish some boundaries between her work and home life. She decides to check her emails at specific times of the day rather than checking them constantly and only checks at home when she is on call. She tries some relaxation techniques to help her to sleep and she asks one of her close friends to meet with her each week to do something they enjoy. They used to meet regularly in the past until Louise said she didn't have enough time anymore. Over time Louise begins to feel the benefits of her actions and her work/life balance improves.

Mindfulness

Having established that professional practice is often stressful and demanding, an understanding of mindfulness and its benefits can be helpful. Unless we are careful, professional life can become a kind of 'pressure cooker' where the steam builds up and needs to be released or it will explode! Mindfulness techniques can help some people to manage stress and take a more deliberate and relaxed approach to their work and life, but like many other approaches it does not offer a solution for everyone. If you are finding the demands of professional practice in any way overwhelming, it is probably worth looking at the area of mindfulness to see if you find it helpful. Whether you decide to adopt it as a lifestyle, select parts that you feel are useful, or reject it completely is, of course, an individual choice. Personally, it took me a long time to learn that I achieve far more when I am relaxed and focused than when I am feeling stressed and tense. At times of high stress I find it far too easy to succumb to feelings of panic, which in turn make me forget things. It is particularly unhelpful when I am panicking about doing something, only to realise I have done it already and then forgotten. To find that I have done something twice at busy times is particularly frustrating!

Williams and Penman (2011) discuss a wide range of issues related to stress that can have an impact on our personal and professional effectiveness, particularly as the demands of professional practice seem to continuously increase. For example, they speak of 'chasing our tails'; when we are very busy we feel we should be doing more or coping better with our workload. As a result, we stay late to try and cope with the volume of work, but when we go home we find it difficult to 'switch off'. We go to bed, but cannot sleep, so we get up the next day and feel tired. Our level of tiredness means that we achieve less at work and so the pressure mounts and our effectiveness decreases. Many of us live our lives on some kind of autopilot as our minds operate in 'doing mode'. We have a lot to do, so we do many things automatically and habitually. This way of living is important as it means that we do not have to think in detail about each aspect of our everyday lives, which would be exhausting. However, if we are in this mode all the time, we overlook the things that bring us pleasure and make us content. We can 'run around' trying to do more and more to keep up, caused, for example, by the guilt that comes from feeling that we are not doing enough, and we omit the things we enjoy in our constant activity. Before long we are living our lives on autopilot and in a metaphorical maze that we cannot find our way out of; as a result, life literally can pass us by.

I have often been asked if it is possible to over think – my immediate response to this is a definite yes. As someone with a strong Reflector style (Honey and Mumford, 2000), I suffer from this frequently and can sometimes feel that my head is literally full as my thoughts race around competing with each other for my attention. Williams and Penman (2011) discuss this particular issue and others in a number of ways in their work on mindfulness. They put forward their model for Mindfulness-Based Cognitive Therapy (MBCT), which has been developed during research in a wide range of situations with large numbers of people, many of whom have found it helpful in the area of managing stress. One of the many benefits of mindfulness techniques is the avoidance of over thinking.

Williams and Penman's (2011) mindfulness programme can be done on an individual basis over a period of eight weeks. As part of it they include a number of exercises in meditation to help individuals to slow down and take stock of what is happening around them, along with 'habit releasers' to take them away from their 'autopilot'. The early part of the book emphasises the importance of breathing exercises that help people to relax, and the suggestion is that these are done each day at specific times, but also as and when needed. The programme builds as the weeks progress; if at any point you feel exhausted and overwhelmed by work, you might find this approach helpful.

'Sharpening the saw'

In this final section we consider Covey's (2004) important concept of 'sharpening the saw'. Irrespective of your particular occupational sector, professional life is always busy and demanding. As a result, it is important to make sure that we take time for ourselves in order to ensure that we are able to perform to the best of our abilities in the interest of our clients and colleagues.

In his best seller *The 7 Habits of Highly Effective People*, Covey (2004) uses the metaphor of 'sharpening the saw' to illustrate this point very effectively. In short, no lumberjack would ever dream of trying to chop down trees without sharpening their saw first. It would be too slow, too difficult and exhausting. In a metaphorical sense, many professionals do just that; they try and manage busy schedules and heavy workloads without taking any time for themselves to 'sharpen their saw'.

Covey suggests that we pay attention to four key areas when sharpening our saw:

1   The physical dimension – caring for our physical bodies, e.g. eating a healthy diet, getting enough sleep, exercising on a regular basis.
2   The spiritual dimension – Covey describes this as our core, centre and commitment to our value system. This is a very private area of life and very individual. It involves spending time drawing on the sources that inspire and uplift us.
3   The mental dimension – caring for our minds and keeping them stimulated, for example reading, continuing in education.
4   The social/emotional dimension – taking time to work at relationships with key people at home and at work.

We can hear many people saying things like 'I would love to do X, but I just don't have the time'. Our lives are so full, however, so the only time we have is the time we make.

Reflective activity 11.5

How do you 'sharpen' your 'saw'?

Case study 11.5

Alfred is a senior manager in a demanding role working for a local authority. As part of his job he is asked to attend a three-day quality management course where he meets people in similar roles. He confides to one course member that he feels that his life is completely out of balance. He says he works all the time, staying late in the office each evening and taking work home with him at the weekends. He describes his life as being in crisis. He senses that his marriage is breaking down and his teenage children complain that he works all the time and never spends any time with them. He says that he knows he has to do something and uses the train journey home from the course to decide what to do. Three months later he attends a review day and the person he confided in is keen to know how things have been since their three-day course. Alfred explains that he went home and explained to his family what he wanted to do. He said that from Monday to Friday he would give his job that he loves his all. He would go in early and stay late most days. However, at the weekends he would do no work at all. Instead, they would do things together as a family, such as watching his son play football, going to see a film and helping with the food shopping and some housework. When asked what the impact of this has been he said that it was unbelievable. He feels much better and his family are all much happier too. But the thing that amazes him most is that he now gets through more work. This is because he now feels refreshed when he goes to work on a Monday morning instead of feeling exhausted.

Conclusion

This chapter began with a review of the terms critically reflective practice and reflexivity. We then explored some key elements of the work of Johns and Brookfield, an exploration of the areas of managing stress, mindfulness and Covey's concept of 'sharpening the saw'. The next and final chapter summarises some of the key perspectives in the book and looks forward to a continuing goal of personal and professional effectiveness.

References

Allen, D. (2002) *Getting Things Done: How to Achieve Stress-Free Productivity*, London: Piatkus Books.
Brookfield, S.D. (1995) *Becoming a Critically Reflective Teacher*, San Francisco: Jossey-Bass.
Covey, S. (2004) *The 7 Habits of Highly Effective People*, London: Pocket Books.
Drucker, Peter (2011) *High Time for Think Time*. Available from www.druckerinstitute.com/2011/high-time-for-think-time/. Accessed 7 May 2015.

Fay, B. (1987) *Critical Social Science*, Cambridge: Polity Press.

Finlay, L. (2008) 'Reflecting on reflective practice', PBPL paper 52, Milton Keynes: Open University.

Fontana, D. (1989) *Managing Stress*, London: BPS Books with Routledge.

Fook, J. and Askeland, G.A. (2006) 'The "critical" in critical reflection', in S. White, J. Fook and F. Gardner (eds) *Critical Reflection in Health and Social Care*, Maidenhead: Open University Press/McGraw-Hill Education.

Honey, P. and Mumford, A. (2000) *The Learning Styles Helper's Guide*, Maidenhead: Peter Honey Publications.

Johns, C. (2013) *Becoming a Reflective Practitioner*, Oxford: Wiley-Blackwell.

Klobassa, V. (2014) 'Activity XXII: Understanding and Attending to Classroom Dynamics: Using the Critical Incident Questionnaire When Teaching Race' in K. Haltinner (ed) Teaching Race and Anti-Racism in Contemporary America, New York: Springer, 328–30.

Kolb, D. (1984) *Experiential Learning: Experience as the Source of Learning and Development*, New Jersey: Prentice Hall.

Lindenfield, G. (2001) *Assert Yourself*, London: Thorsons.

Loughran, J.J. (2002) 'Effective reflective practice: in search of meaning in learning about teaching', *Journal of Teacher Education*, 53(1), 33–43.

Schön, D.A. (1983) *The Reflective Practitioner*, Aldershot: Ashgate.

Thompson, N. (2012) *Anti Discriminatory Practice*, 5th edn, Basingstoke: Palgrave Macmillan.

Thompson, S. and Thompson, N. (2008) *The Critically Reflective Practitioner*, Basingstoke: Palgrave Macmillan.

Williams, M. and Penman, D. (2011) *Mindfulness: A Practical Guide to Finding Peace in a Frantic World*, London: Piatkus.

12 Review and looking forward

'It is a most mortifying reflection for a man to consider what he has done, compared to what he might have done.'

(Samuel Johnson)

Introduction

In this final chapter we will review our journey through this book, using the Integrated Reflective Cycle (Bassot, 2013) to summarise some of the concepts covered and to draw some of the key threads together. We will then look forward to the kind of practitioners we want to become and how we might achieve this. Central to this will be Senge's (2006) concept of Personal Mastery and the need to ensure there is creative tension in our practice to maintain momentum and to keep us moving forward. The chapter will conclude with some key questions for continued reflection.

Review and the Integrated Reflective Cycle

In this book we have made a journey from the foundations of reflective practice to critically reflective practice where critical reflection is so integrated in our professional lives that it becomes our way of being. We have examined a number of theoretical concepts along the way and I hope that you have engaged with some of the activities suggested in each chapter. Hopefully the case studies have resonated with some of your own particular professional practice and have also given you insights into the practice of people in other professions.

Our journey began with a discussion of what reflective practice is and the need for practitioners to reflect on their practice. We then explored a range of seminal literature on reflective practice, which helps us to learn from our professional experience by evaluating it in order to develop and improve it. We then progressed towards our destination of critically reflective practice by examining the place of feelings in professional practice, followed by a critical consideration of how we make assumptions and the importance of challenging these in order to practice in an anti discriminatory way. We then looked at learning from feedback and how we can reflect effectively in groups. As we began to look forward we considered the management of change and how critical reflection can be integrated into our lives as a way of being.

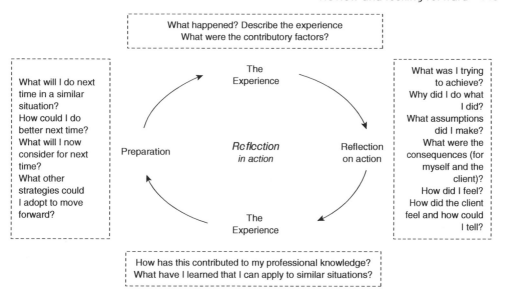

Figure 12.1 The Integrated Reflective Cycle

My own Integrated Reflective Cycle (Bassot, 2013) is shown above and draws on some of the key literature covered in the book. It is always useful to compare and contrast different theoretical approaches, as they often have their relative strengths and weaknesses. In this cycle I have highlighted the strengths of a number of theoretical approaches and have posed questions around the cycle in order to help your continued thinking.

Reflective activity 12.1

Examine the Integrated Cycle – which theoretical approaches can you find within it?

Taking a questioning approach to professional practice is an excellent way of delving deeper into not only what you did, but why; this is a key feature of critically reflective practice. Clearly The Integrated Cycle is not completely new and this cycle (like many others that we have discussed) draws on the work of Kolb (1984). It also uses some of the questions posed by Gibbs (1998) and Johns (2009).

The cycle starts with an experience; we are encouraged to describe what happened but also to think about the context of the experience. This, of course, can have a major impact on how we view the experience and what we do in the particular situation. It also asks us to examine the contributory factors, some of which might stem from the past (for example, our previous experiences) and the present.

We are then asked to reflect-on-action (Schön, 1983) in order to interrogate our approach. This includes an examination of the feelings we experienced and any assumptions we might be making. In addition, we are asked to think about the possible consequences of these assumptions and how the client might have experienced things too.

We then examine how this experience can contribute to our professional knowledge; for example, what can we learn from it that we could later apply to other similar situations. And what is new that we can add to what we already know? What is different that we need to recognise and pay attention to?

The final step on the cycle asks us to look forward to see how we might use this knowledge and experience in the future. Here, it is important to consider the strategies that could be adopted next time.

Reflection-in-action is shown in the centre of the cycle; this emphasises that this kind of 'thinking on our feet' is constant and needs to be done throughout the experience.

Case study 12.1

Katy is a counsellor in private practice who values spending time reflecting on her practice. She is currently working with a 17-year-old student (Amy) who has been self-harming and, following one of her sessions, she uses the questions on the Integrated Reflective Cycle to help her to examine her practice.

The experience – Amy seemed very distressed today. She told me that she has been self-harming again. I suppose exam time is coming round soon, which always seems to put her under lots of pressure. She always wants to do well and to make her parents happy. Deep down she knows she is scared of failing.

Reflection-on-action – I want to support Amy and try to help her to see more of why she self-harms. I felt really upset when she told me she had cut herself again, particularly as it's been quite a while since she's done this. I suppose I'd assumed that she'd be all right, particularly because we talked about the stress of exams coming up the last time we met. She's such an able student and I wish she could see how capable she really is. Instead, she always seems so hard on herself. As soon as she walked through the door I could see that she was in a bad way. Her whole demeanour was very subdued.

Theory – so what can I learn from all of this? I can see that self-harming is something that can rear its ugly head again and again when people feel their life is getting out of control and when they are overwhelmed by their emotions. Getting to know Amy is helping me to understand more about the pressures young people can experience.

Preparation – Working with Amy has helped me to understand more about self-harming and I can see that I need to read more about it. I've also seen a training day being offered by a charity that specialises in supporting those who are self-harming, so I will register for that, which should help.

Like any other model, The Integrated Reflective Cycle should be critiqued as it also has its relative strengths and weaknesses. Critiquing any theory and in particular its relationship to professional practice is always necessary in order to identify its strengths and weaknesses. Strengths in theoretical approaches are the things that help you to develop your understandings and to take your practice forward; weaknesses are the aspects that could hinder your progress and which you might want to discard. It is always important to be clear about the reasons for your critique and to make sure that you can justify your arguments. For example, using a model just because you like it might not be a decision you can easily defend. In the same way, discarding something only because it takes you into difficult territory is also questionable. It is important to remember that critically reflective practice asks us to accept a level of 'inner discomfort' (Boyd and Fales, 1983: 106) so that our practice can develop. You could critique The Integrated Cycle by posing questions such as 'Can I only start at the top of the cycle, or could I begin at any point? The arrows only point in one direction; could I travel round the cycle in the opposite direction, or even track across the cycle?'

Senge's concept of personal mastery

In his book *The Fifth Discipline*, Senge (2006) discusses his concept of personal mastery, which is an enlightening way of considering our continuous professional development. Personal mastery is more than being competent and skilful and involves living life from a creative viewpoint rather than a reactive one. Senge describes personal mastery as a discipline with two continuous processes. First, we have to clarify what is important to us in our work; this means having a vision for our practice. Without a vision, we do not know where we are heading or what we are aiming for. Second, we should seek to see our current reality more clearly, so that we can begin to move towards our vision.

Reflective activity 12.2

Now think about your vision for your practice and write down a statement in a few sentences that encapsulates what you are aiming for in your professional life and the kind of practitioner you would like to be. It is useful to think of a vision as a destination. If this is difficult, imagine you hear your colleagues talking about you in a very positive way. What do you hope they would be saying?

Creative tension is the force between our vision and our current reality. Now imagine stretching an elastic band between your two hands, with one hand above the other. The hand above is your vision and the hand below is your current reality. The elastic band stretched between the two represents the creative tension between your vision and your current reality. This creative tension is central to Senge's concept of personal mastery as it is this force that moves us forward towards our vision.

Tension is a word that usually has negative connotations associated with stress and distress. Creative tension, however, is a positive term and is the source of creative energy that we need to continue learning and developing. It enables our practice to keep moving forward and is vital in retaining a high level of motivation and commitment to professional practice.

In the image of the elastic band outlined above there are, of course, two possible movements that can happen. First, I hold on to my vision, keeping the upper hand in place, and my current reality then moves up towards my vision. Or, second, I lose sight of my vision and the upper hand moves down towards the acceptance of my current reality. It is also important to remember that, as my current reality moves towards my vision, my vision must continue to move forward or the creative tension will be lost. Vision, therefore, is not a permanent or static concept but one that is continually changing and moving forward. People who show a high level of personal mastery continually review their vision in order to maintain the creative tension needed to move forward through a continuous process of learning.

People who show a high level of personal mastery demonstrate the following characteristics:

- They have a special sense of purpose that some would articulate as a calling.
- They see their current reality as an ally not an enemy.
- They work with the forces of change not against them.
- They are deeply inquisitive.
- They feel connected with others.
- They are aware of their uniqueness.
- They feel part of a creative process.
- They are always learning.
- They are aware of what they do not know and where they need to grow and develop.
- They view mistakes as opportunities for growth.
- They are deeply self-confident.

Case study 12.2

Julian is an Economics teacher in a secondary school. He went into teaching after a career in banking because he no longer found the work stimulating. He felt that he would gain more satisfaction from working with young people and wanted an opportunity to give something back to society. Julian's vision for his practice is to be an excellent, caring and compassionate teacher who enables students to grow in their knowledge of Economics and themselves. Ultimately, he wants his students to achieve their full potential and to live successful (however they define success) independent adult lives. He loves teaching Economics because it is a practical subject that can help the students understand the way the world and, in particular, business operates. Julian enjoys keeping up to date with current affairs and reads widely. He regularly discusses economic issues with his students and is known as an inspirational teacher.

By contrast, Senge also describes two kinds of unconscious beliefs that many people have which serve to work against personal mastery. The first is powerlessness; we feel unable to bring about those things that we really care about. The second is unworthiness: that we do not deserve to have what we desire. Most people hold one of these and both work against enabling us to achieve what we really want to achieve. Just as creative tension propels us towards our vision, our feelings of powerlessness and unworthiness hold us back from achieving our vision.

Reflective activity 12.3

Think about the two points above. Does either of them resonate with your own experiences? What is holding you back from realising your vision?

Some final reflections

Having reached the final part of this book, it is good to reflect back as we conclude. Professional practice can be demanding, but as a result is rarely boring. Thinking back on the time since you began reading this book, it is helpful to identify your major learning points. It is also useful to consider how you can continue to move your practice forward. This usually involves considering what you need to learn next. Support from others in your learning is vital in helping you to achieve your potential, so it is worth making sure that you have people around you who can continue to do this, as well as being mindful of those whom you can support too – in my experience, we can learn a lot from supporting others. Looking ahead can help us to think more about our vision, which in turn fosters the creative tension we need to become the professional practitioners we would like to be in the future.

Conclusion

In this chapter we have focused on The Integrated Cycle and Senge's concept of personal mastery. Senge's work reminds us of the importance of continuing to look forward to develop ourselves and our practice in order to achieve our vision. Critically reflective practice enables us to be mindful practitioners who accept nothing at face value. As we continue to examine ourselves and our work in this way, we ensure that we meet the needs of our clients whilst maintaining satisfying and fulfilling working lives.

References

Bassot, B. (2013) *The Reflective Journal*, Basingstoke: Palgrave Macmillan.

Boyd, E.M. and Fales, A.W. (1983) 'Reflective learning: key to learning from experience,' *Journal of Humanistic Psychology*, 23(2), 99–117.

Gibbs, G. (1998) *Learning by Doing: A Guide to Teaching and Learning Methods*, Oxford: Further Education Unit, Oxford Polytechnic.

Johns, C. (2009) *Becoming a Reflective Practitioner*, 3rd edn, Chichester: Wiley-Blackwell.

Kolb, D. (1984) *Experiential Learning: Experience as the Source of Learning and Development*, Upper Saddle River, NJ: Prentice Hall.

Schön, D.A. (1983) *The Reflective Practitioner*, Aldershot: Ashgate.

Senge, P. (2006) *The Fifth Discipline*, 2nd edn, London: Random House Business.

INDEX

Printed in Great Britain
by Amazon

61108017R00095